Correspondence 1949–1975

New Heidegger Research

Series editors:

Gregory Fried, Professor of Philosophy, Suffolk University, USA
Richard Polt, Professor of Philosophy, Xavier University, USA

The *New Heidegger Research* series promotes informed and critical dialogue that breaks new philosophical ground by taking into account the full range of Heidegger's thought, as well as the enduring questions raised by his work.

Titles in the Series:

Correspondence 1949–1975

Martin Heidegger
and
Ernst Jünger

Translated by
Timothy Sean Quinn

ROWMAN & LITTLEFIELD
INTERNATIONAL

London • New York

Published by Rowman & Littlefield International Ltd
Unit A, Whitacre Mews, 26–34 Stannary Street, London SE11 4AB
www.rowmaninternational.com

Rowman & Littlefield International Ltd.is an affiliate of Rowman & Littlefield
4501 Forbes Boulevard, Suite 200, Lanham, Maryland 20706, USA
With additional offices in Boulder, New York, Toronto (Canada), and Plymouth (UK)
www.rowman.com

British Library Cataloguing in Publication Data

A catalogue record for this book is available from the British Library

ISBN: HB 978-1-7834-8875-9
       PB 978-1-7834-8876-6

Library of Congress Cataloging-in-Publication Data

Names: Heidegger, Martin, 1889–1976, author. | Quinn, Timothy Sean,
   translator. | Junger, Ernst, 1895–1998. Uber die Linie. English.
Title: Correspondence, 1949–1975 / Martin Heidegger and Ernst Junger;
   translated by Timothy Sean Quinn.
Description: New York : Rowman & Littlefield International, 2016. | Series:
   New Heidegger research | Description based on print version record and CIP
   data provided by publisher; resource not viewed.
Identifiers: LCCN 2016018572 (print) | LCCN 2016014247 (ebook) | ISBN
   9781783488773 (electronic) | ISBN 9781783488759 (cloth : alk. paper) |
   ISBN 9781783488766 (pbk. : alk. paper)
Subjects: LCSH: Junger, Ernst, 1895–1998—Correspondence. | Authors,
   German—20th century—Correspondence. | Philosophers,
   German—Correspondence.
Classification: LCC PT2619.U43 (print) | LCC PT2619.U43 Z48 2016 (ebook) |
   DDC 838/.91209—dc23
LC record available at https://lccn.loc.gov/2016018572

Printed in the United States of America

To My Family
Kathryn, Ben, Rachel, Máire

Contents

Acknowledgements

I owe a sincere debt of gratitude to Gregory Fried and Richard Polt for encouraging this project, and especially to Richard Polt for his thoughtful criticisms and suggestions for improvement of my translation. I owe thanks as well to Sarah Campbell of Rowman & Littlefield International, as well as to Sinéad Murphy, for their efforts shepherding this book to completion. But for the steady assistance and good advice of all of them, this book would not exist.

Acknowledgements

Translator's Introduction

Beginning in the early 1930s, Martin Heidegger began what would become a life-long engagement with the work of Ernst Jünger, but the two would not formally meet until 1948, at Heidegger's celebrated "hut" in Todtnauberg. One year later, Jünger inaugurated a regular correspondence with Heidegger that lasted until Heidegger's death in 1976. This volume is a translation of that correspondence; it also includes a translation of an essay Jünger composed on the occasion of Heidegger's sixtieth birthday, "Über die Linie" ("Across the Line").[1]

Unlike Heidegger, Ernst Jünger is relatively unknown to English-speaking readers. Yet at the time their correspondence began, Jünger had already established himself in Europe as a preeminent novelist and essayist. His first book, *In Stahlgewittern* (*Storm of Steel*, 1920), was a record of his experiences in the cauldron of World War I. During the 1920s and 1930s, Jünger would publish ten more volumes, offering further reflections on war, but also critiquing the failure of liberal democracy to resist modernity's drift into various forms of totalitarianism. From this period comes the work that first drew Heidegger's attention, *Der Arbeiter* (*The Worker*, 1932). Along with his celebrated military record, Jünger's literary reputation also drew the attention of the National Socialist Party, which continued for a decade to attempt to

---

1. The volume used for this translation is *Ernst Jünger, Martin Heidegger: Briefwechsel 1949–1975*, ed. Günter Figal (Stuttgart: Klett-Cotta, 2008). Jünger's novels and essays are available in twenty-two volumes in his *Sämtliche Werke* (Stuttgart: Klett-Cotta, 1978–2003). There is also a fine French translation of their correspondence by Julien Hervier, *Ernst Jünger, Martin Heidegger, Correspondance 1949–1975* (Paris: Christian Bourgois, 2010).

recruit Jünger to its ranks. Although Jünger was a political conservative linked with other "nationalist" writers, he not only refused the Nazi's solicitations; he published a short and highly allegorical novel, *Auf den Marmorklippen* (*On the Marble Cliffs*, 1939), critical of Hitler's Germany. Nonetheless, during World War II, Jünger served in Paris in an administrative position with the German Army; his reflections on this time are recorded in his book *Gärten und Straßen* (*Gardens and Paths*, 1942). As a German officer associated with conservative politics, but at the same time opposed to the Nazi Party, Jünger found himself on the periphery of the plot led by Claus von Stauffenberg to assassinate Hitler. Nevertheless, he was not directly implicated, suffering only dismissal from the army. After the war, Jünger continued his prolific career, authoring over forty more books before his death in 1998.

According to Heidegger, an admiring but critical study of two of Jünger's writings, the essay "Total Mobilization" of 1930 and the book *The Worker* of 1932, framed that most controversial decade of his career. What impressed Heidegger in these works was "how they express an essential understanding of Nietzsche's metaphysics, insofar as the history and the present of the Western world are seen and foreseen within the horizon of this metaphysics." From Jünger, Heidegger learned "the universal rule of the will to power within planetary history. Today everything is a part of this reality, whether it is called communism, or fascism, or world democracy."[2] Jünger's Nietzschean judgments concerning the development of nihilism in Europe subsequently help to inspire a series of essays from Heidegger: they are at work especially (although unacknowledged) in "The Question Concerning Technology."[3]

---

2. Martin Heidegger, *Gesamtausgabe* (GA), vol. 16 (Frankfurt am Main: Vittorio Klostermann, 2004), 375. Heidegger reports, in a reflection from 1945 (*Das Rektorat 1933/34: Tatsachen und Gedanken*, GA 16: 375), that he studied Jünger in a small reading group with his assistant Werner Brock (1901–1974). The results of his lifelong engagement with Jünger compose GA 90, "Zu Ernst Jünger." Excerpts from GA 90 have been translated in *The Heidegger Reader*, edited by Günter Figal (Bloomington: Indiana University Press, 2009), trans. Jerome Veith, pp. 189–206.

3. *The Question Concerning Technology and Other Essays* (New York and London: Garland Publishing, 1977). See also Rüdiger Safranski, *Ein Meister aus Deutschland: Heidegger und seine Zeit* (Frankfurt am Main: Fischer Taschenbuch Verlag, 1977), 329. See also Heidegger's remarks in "On the Question of Being,"

At the same time, however, Heidegger was critical of Jünger. Concerning what he called Jünger's "bedazzlement" (*Blendung*) and "blindness" (*Verblendung*) before the thought of Nietzsche, Heidegger judges that Jünger fails to see the "essence and ground of the contemporary subjectivity of humanity" and therewith "the authentic sphere of decision . . . between Being and beings."[4]

In 1949, Jünger inaugurated what would become a regular correspondence with Heidegger to solicit Heidegger's interest in the possibilities of founding a new journal titled *Pallas*. As the correspondence reveals, though, Heidegger chose to retreat from public involvements, in so far as that was possible for him to manage, and in general remained somewhat dismissive of politics.

Jünger's admiration for Heidegger is clear throughout their correspondence. Heidegger, for his part, is respectful to Jünger, writing tenderly on the occasion of the death of Jünger's first wife.[5] Also, Heidegger shows Jünger the rare honor of including him posthumously in a special mailing, sent only to family members and close friends, of verses from Hölderlin that Heidegger selected to share only after his death.[6]

The core of their friendship, however, turns on their shared attitude toward modernity and to the growing nihilism of the age. The touchstone for this issue is Jünger's *The Worker*, which remained salient for Heidegger throughout his life.[7] It is, too, as "the germ of a newer version" of *The Worker* that Heidegger understood Jünger's essay "Across the Line," a work that "once again" brought the themes of *The Worker* to "the consciousness of the age." Jünger composed this essay as a contribution to a *Festschrift* for Heidegger's sixtieth birthday. The essay is significant for two reasons in particular. First, it represents Jünger's recovery, in the aftermath of World War II, of themes he developed extensively between World Wars I and II. Second, "Across the Line" elicited from Heidegger a significant response: an essay later

in *Pathmarks*, ed. William MacNeill (Cambridge: Cambridge University Press, 1998), 295.

4. GA 90: 13–14.
5. Heidegger to Jünger, 22 November 1960.
6. Elfride Heidegger to Jünger, 16 June 1976.
7. Jünger to Heidegger, 27 November 1967.

published as a book with the title *Zur Seinsfrage* (*On The Question of Being*), but initially given a title by Heidegger that puns on the title of Jünger's essay: "Über 'die Linie'" ("About 'The Line'").[8]

The principal theme of Jünger's essay is the abolition of nihilism. Jünger devotes the majority of his essay to what he calls "diagnostic remarks" about nihilism's main features. Following Nietzsche, Jünger judges the root of these symptoms to be "the decline of values . . . above all the decline of Christian values."

There is, however, a deeper issue involved with the nihilistic diagnosis: the impossibility of representing Nothing. One response to this circumstance has been an identification of nihilism with chaos or with disease. From Jünger's point of view, it is neither. Indeed, "with a bit of observation one will find that physical health is connected with it—above all where it is vigorously at work" (§8).

Finally, Jünger notes that nihilism is not a species of evil: "programs of nihilistic action can be distinguished by good intentions and philanthropy," specifically as antidote to emergent political disorder. "The nihilist is no criminal in the traditional sense," Jünger writes; he is, instead, one who abandons any distinction between good and evil, a situation Jünger deems "more disturbing" than explicit criminality (§10).

Among the principal symptoms of nihilistic reductionism is the turn toward method and toward specialization in the sciences. In the arts, a similar reductionism occurs. Nihilism, in Jünger's view, characterized by its symptomatic reductionisms, its shrinking of human values, its transformation of the citizen into the worker, has become the norm. We have reached, in his words, "the null point." Jünger therefore asks: do there exist at this null point any signs of hope? Is even "a restricted scope of freedom possible" (§20)? Yes, he answers; there are "oases in our deserts," two in particular: poetry and eros. Poet and thinker, Jünger writes, stand in "mirror-like correspondence" (§21). Both are able to confront nothingness without being overwhelmed by it.

It is necessary to raise the question concerning Jünger's own activity as "poet and thinker" in relation to his age: is his own act of writing a "crossing of the line" or but the final symptom of nihilism's progress

---

8. Heidegger, *Pathmarks*, 291.

toward the null point? This question would inform Heidegger's response to Jünger, in the essay *"Über 'die Linie.'"*

A NOTE ON THE TRANSLATION

In Heidegger's letter responding to Jünger's essay "Across the Line," I have chosen to render the word *Zuwendung* as "turning approach," rather than the more literal "turning" or "turning-toward," in order to distinguish it from the word *Kehre* or "turning," which is customarily understood to announce a shift of emphasis in Heidegger's thinking in the aftermath of *Being and Time*.[9] In the context in which Jünger and Heidegger use it here, *Zuwendung* has the sense of a turning that invites a corresponding notice or response, a turning-toward that is also an invitation. "Turning approach," while not at all perfect, intends to capture this sense of the word while simultaneously avoiding confusion with *die Kehre*.

I have rendered the word *über* in the title of Jünger's essay as "across," rather than as "over" or "above," in order to connect it with Heidegger's criticism of Jünger's view of the location of nihilism in *"Über 'die Linie.'"* There, Heidegger considers nihilism not as a line to be crossed but as a "zone" or region we inhabit. "Across" therefore seemed a more fitting translation than "over," even though that sense of the word remains at work as well in both Jünger's essay and in Heidegger's response.

Finally, I have chosen to preserve the German *Herr* rather than translating it "Mr." in the salutations of the correspondence.

---

9. Heidegger to Jünger, 18 December 1950.

Part One

THE CORRESPONDENCE BETWEEN ERNST JÜNGER AND MARTIN HEIDEGGER

Correspondence Between Ernst Jünger and Martin Heidegger

1) Ernst Jünger to Martin Heidegger, (14b)
Ravensburg, Wilhelm-Hauff-Strasse 18,
11 June 1949

Dear Herr Professor,

Herr Klett and Dr. Nebel have informed me about their correspondence with you.[1] Although I welcome the plan for a journal and for the editorial committee they have in view, I also understand your reservations, thanks to similarities to my own situation. The fact of a collaboration, or even working in common, seems unobjectionable to me; on the other hand, I regard granting an official status to this common work, either on the title page, or through an advertisement, as a step worth being weighed for a long time, and perhaps reserved for a later stage. I responded in this way to Herr Klett, and have included a copy of my response for you. I think my brother shares this opinion. We all find ourselves in a situation where it is fitting to offer to the polemic only material that is absolutely necessary. In any case, things must be considered carefully, since much depends on them. It is necessary to give preference to points of view that favor the work of the collaborator.

---

1. Gerhard Nebel (1903–1974) was a publisher and conservative essayist who had studied with Heidegger in the 1920s. He met Jünger in 1941 while serving in Paris as an interpreter with the Luftwaffe, where he frequented the "Stefan Georg Circle" that included a number of German officers opposed to Hitler. After the war, he undertook a defense of Jünger in his book *Ernst Jünger. Abenteurer des Geistes* (*Ernst Jünger: Adventurer of the Spirit.* [Wuppertal: Marées-Verlag, 1949]).

I hope that you are enjoying this lovely season from your high locale. For my part, I am content with having moved to Ravensburg, where I can work well. In addition, leaving the English zone for the French, one has the feeling of entering into the sphere of a cultivated nation, in spite of all the cosmetic deficiencies that are inevitably tied up with an occupation.

With best wishes

Yours,

E. J.

[the following letter was included by Ernst Jünger]

Ernst Jünger (14b) Ravensburg, Wilhelm-Hauff-Strasse 18, 11 June 1949

Dear Herr Klett,

I gratefully received your kind letter of 7 June. I am therefore ready for our trip into streams of Mexican colors, and I ask you to proceed with all necessary preparations with Dr. Frederking.[2] Naturally, it will be necessary to avoid turning the thing into a folk festival. The great room of Pastor Gestrich seems to me entirely suitable for the experience.

I am grateful for the paper; the most practical format for me would be that of the sheet on which I now write.

Dr. Nebel kept me posted about your correspondence with Professor Heidegger. My brother Friedrich Georg, who actually stayed in Hirschberg at the Countess Podewils's, has yet to give me a definitive answer.[3] The reservations Professor Heidegger expresses are not unfounded; they tally in part with mine, which I've explained to you and to Dr. Nebel. Heidegger and I have found ourselves for the past four years at the center of an intense polemic, and have indeed survived it; but it is important that we in no way offer a larger target to our adversaries. I believe that Professor Heidegger has as little to fear from a substantial statement as do I, but that he must dispel any suspicion of

2. In January 1950, Jünger and Ernst Klett took mescaline under the supervision of the psychiatrist Walter Frederking.

3. The Countess Sophie Dorothee von Podewils (1909–1979), born von Hirschberg, was a poet and novelist married to Clemens von Podewils, a journalist who maintained a close friendship with Ernst Jünger and his brother, Friedrich Georg.

political action. The publication of a journal would however be considered in a political light, whether we intend it or not—here as well as abroad. I would still prefer then, that Dr. Nebel assume sole editorial responsibility and that we however assist by collaborating with him, which would also please my brother. The effect remains the same, but this reduces the possibilities for attack. If each of the principal collabo-rators declared themselves prepared to give a contribution to the first number, the launch would be assured, and the journal would receive a definite look. There would always be time to institute a closer collabo-ration once the necessary authority had been assured of the quality of the magazine and its audience. Indeed, I assume a stream of new and even as yet unknown collaborators. This is the position in which I find myself, and which requires that the right thing be a calm and precise action. I suggest then that you initially approach the other gentlemen from the point of view of a permanent collaboration, based solely on regular participation. For my part, I am entirely prepared. Hopefully, the common work will drive further efforts.

So much in brief. I do hope to see you next month. Concerning Herr Hiller, more time is needed.[4] Perhaps one day you could command Nebel like a new Odysseus against this Thersites.[5] I hold Hiller as one of those principally responsible for the Jewish pogroms; it was he who furnished material for the *Stürmer* by besmirching everything German for decades. Hiller and Streicher, they are two sides of the same coin, and I hold it superfluous for you to answer such men with arguments.[6]

With best wishes,

Yours,

E. J.

---

4. Kurt Hiller (1885–1972), a German essayist, political pacifist, and early defender of gay rights. Imprisoned by the Nazis in a variety of concentration camps between 1933–1934, he eventually fled Germany for Prague (1934) and then London (1938). At a conference in London of 20 October 1945, he said of Jünger: "Noble nationalist literature, more discreet, more politic, more civilized, is more dangerous at a distance. Ernst Jünger is more dangerous than Adolf Hitler; Thomas Mann's *Thoughts of an Apolitical Man* are more dangerous than Jünger."

5. See *Iliad* Book II. 211–77. Thersites attempts to agitate the Greek armies to oppose Agamemnon and return to Greece; Odysseus severely reprimands him.

6. Julius Streicher (1885–1946), founder of the Nazi journal *Der Stürmer* and an advocate of anti-Semitic violence. He was condemned at Nuremberg for crimes against humanity, and executed in 1946.

2) Martin Heidegger to Ernst Jünger, Freiburg-in-Breslau, 23 June 1949

Dear Herr Jünger,

I thank you for your letter that aligns with my own reflections. But first I must ask that you drop the "Professor."

I still recall well the location of the path on which we spoke last autumn about the extreme danger that faces those who try today to hold onto what is essential; that to endure solitude is not an escape, but the highest freedom.

Yet the natural urge to bring help immediately, to offer support and guidance, moves us to attempt things that turn out to be wrong after more rigorous reflection.

Since Herr Klett and Dr. Nebel came to see me, not a day passes when I do not reflect on the project. The will to discover and to make visible in an original way what is authentic in the western tradition, to gather together those who wait, to strengthen those who seek, is enchanting. But, as I see clearly today, all this goes down the path of a relapse into the worn-out form of the journal. The tyranny of public opinion cannot be broken within it. The joint appearance of our names, even under the simple form of a regular collaboration, would be transformed into a political event that would perhaps either shake our last secure position, or in the end confuse it.

There is a posthumous note of Nietzsche's with which you're certainly acquainted, from the time of the *Gay Science*: "Venice is formed by a hundred profound solitudes together—that is her magic. An image of the man of the future."[7]

It seems to me that a law for future poets and thinkers hides here, for whose preparatory practice we are perhaps appointed.

That is why I think we should retreat from this project and allow its fate to mature longer. We should not throw the last scraps to the persistent thirst for vengeance, which has in the meantime become more crafty; we must remain unassailable in what is proper for us. The best tactic would not at all help; we have been overtaken tactically for a long time. A few days ago, my friend, a refugee from Upper Silesia who lives with us, received a letter from a Jewish émigré (a professor in the

---

7. Friedrich Nietzsche, *Die Fröliche Wissenschaft*, in *Sämtliche Werke*, ed. Giorgio Colli and Mazzino Montinari, Kritische Studienausgabe, vol. 3 (Berlin/New York: de Gruyter, 1880), 343–651.

USA) who wrote that he (that is, is to say, "one" [*d.h. man*]) is extremely anxious to learn what was going on with Jünger's and Heidegger's new journal.[8]

I am pleased that you feel at home in Upper Swabia, a land I love, and I hope that I can visit you there one day. We leave at the end of the week for the hut, which is no longer so weatherproof.

Cordially,

Yours,

Martin Heidegger

3) Ernst Jünger to Martin Heidegger, Ravensburg, Wilhelm Hauff-Strasse 18, 25 June 1949

Dear Herr Heidegger,

Your judgment of the situation comes across as quite correct. The idea of constituting an organ for the last independent thinkers and creators was somewhat attractive. But it would perhaps have led to a stronger investment than was the intention of the participants. In the course of the last year it became entirely clear to me that silence is the strongest weapon, providing that something hides itself behind it that is worth being hushed up.

I will happily come up when I have the chance, perhaps in the company of Friedrich Georg or Vittorio Klostermann. At the moment, I am submerged in work on old and new manuscripts.

Cordially,

Yours,

Ernst Jünger

4) Ernst Jünger to Martin Heidegger, Ravensburg, 6 January 1950

Dear Herr Heidegger,

Once again I have to thank you for the gift of your "The Country

---

8. The reference is probably to Hans Jonas (1903–1993), a student of Husserl and Heidegger, who fled Germany in 1933 for England and then for Palestine. Teaching in Canada and finally at the New School for Social Research in New York City, he is the author of several books concerning Gnosticism, technology, and the philosophy of biology.

Path."⁹ This gift has offered me new insights into the nature of your thinking.

As our common editor Vittorio Klostermann has reported to you, I wish to express to you my thanks, not only for your gift, but for your existence, by means of a contribution to the *Festschrift* that will appear on the occasion of your jubilee. The contribution would perhaps not be homogeneous with the others, but on the other hand, hopefully, genuine.

From Herr Barth, one of my readers, I received a detailed account of your visit to Bremen.¹⁰ I don't know whether the discussion he reported is sufficient in its details. It struck me that you have spoken of "my" new theology—in any event, it is an ambition to which I do not aspire. What unsettles me much more is the absence of any profound theological analysis, which I hope philosophers will put right; this is a task that neither the philosopher nor the poet could evade, not to mention entirely independent of other forces.

Further, concerning myself, I do not claim to be a Christian. Even less, an anti-Christian. In this respect, there seems to reside a significant antagonism in your statements. I would rather prefer to remain favorable and wait and see, appreciating the facts. The churches have absorbed many of the shocks we have experienced. Even today, in a town like Ravensburg, were the two confessions there to disappear, cannibalism would break out overnight. It sits beneath a thin veneer.

I grant that these are still things one can appreciate *post festum*. But who knows whether in some inaccessible supernatural world, there is not already, among others, a Christian age seeking to be born? Perhaps the preliminary events that are coming to pass there will become manifest even in our lifetime. Heaven seems like an eggshell that just needs one last peck.

I have abandoned the plan for a journal. I recognize how correct your hesitations were, in particular, in view of the new press campaign that is underway against me. Many people find that I menace their security. Certainly, such a forum for clarifying issues such as these would have

---

9. *Der Feldweg*, GA: 13, 87–90.

10. Heinrich Barth (1914–1997), lawyer and politician who served in the Adenauer administration.

been good, but it is better to stay away from conversation with the "lemurs."[11]

Cordially,

Yours,

E. J.

5) Martin Heidegger to Ernst Jünger, Freiburg im Breisgau, 18 December 1950

Dear Herr Jünger,

My heartfelt thanks, arriving scandalously late, for your "contribution."[12] "Across the Line" is a stimulating venture in which you take part immediately in Being itself. Your contribution, like your brother's, is in this way essentially distinguished from all the other contributions. At the same time it expresses an encouraging affinity for walking "off the beaten track" that you illuminate clearly.[13]

The spirit that was already active in *The Worker*, but which, in a certain way, still remained tied there to a fixed reality, is now purified, its vision widened, and, above all, has gained in prescience and, ready to assist, is freely on the way.

This writing brings to young people a beautiful initiation in a seeing that is not limited to an analysis of the situation, and then coupled with instructions for how to act. The seeing is itself a crossing of the line.

But above all, this presumed demand also restores a desperate courage to those who still manage "the unknown capital of suffering" (258, 274). They are often reduced to clumsy attempts, within an environment that would still like to be furnished in long-fragmented modes of representation.

As I read your "contribution" for the first time—I read it first, before the others—I was, aside from the well-traversed path, especially

---

11. In Jünger's terminology, "lemurs" represent bureaucratic, dictatorial officials.

12. The reference is to the collection of essays published in honor of Heidegger's sixtieth birthday: *Anteile. Martin Heidegger zum 60. Geburtstag* (Frankfurt am Main: Klostermann, 1950).

13. The phrase "off the beaten track" alludes to Heidegger's book *Holzwege*, GA: 5.

pleased, since I could say to myself that you yourself have already
attained freedom and superiority in relation to *The Worker*, which
allows you to bring that work once again to the consciousness of the
age. You know from our first conversation on the way to Stübenwasen,
how much this work means to me. Yet perhaps "Across the Line" is
the germ of a newer version, in style and dimension, of *The Worker*.

That is why I would still like to indicate my particular interest in
your "contribution" by means of some questions.

I find the metaphysical kernel on the bottom of page 271: "The
moment in which the line is passed brings a new turning approach
(*Zuwendung*) of Being. . . ." Must we not, in order to respond to the
essence of Being, at the same time say: the line is first passable in the
moment instigated by Being in its turning approach, which turning
approach is first an awakening and eventful addressing of the essence
of man?

The crossing of the line that unfolds in proximity to nothingness is
no mere advance of man. It is at the same time an *over*taking by what
saves, whose beyond first genuinely illuminates the line for the crossing
over. It seems necessary to me to keep this in view in order to acquire
the purity of your style for this path.

In that direction two questions preoccupy me. They lead to articu-
lating the extremely important distinctions between nihilism as a
"fundamental power" and chaos, illness, and evil. Without clarifying
these relations, "theology" in particular gropes about in the fog.

If however the fundamental power of nihilism and therewith "the
line" are not symptoms of an illness, then the thinking that goes beyond
the line still remains inadequate to its object, as long as it is grouped
under medical terms of prognosis, diagnosis, and therapy. Clearly, it
could be that you have chosen this classification simply because the
inevitable limitations of your contribution demand it. I know that you
are far from elevating psychotherapy to *the* metaphysics of the age.
Because, nevertheless, the modes of representation converge there and
thus promote a new and dangerous anthropology, it would be necessary
to stem the tide. To be sure, there is a plan of the young Nietzsche from
the year 1873, for a text whose title would be: "The philosopher as the
physician of culture."

My second question concerns the notion of "order." You show
clearly that even in nihilism order reigns (253), that it even belongs to

its style (256). On the other hand, you state (250) that on this side of the line is found no "supreme thought of order," any more than "the perfect work of art." Even beyond the line you retain order as a fundamental category, and you distinguish only by degrees between order on this side of the line and across the line. It seems to me that the line would be the boundary for an essential distinction, not finite but infinite. The category of order is still a relic of the ungrounded form-matter relation, in any event, in which all dialectic moves, whether idealistic or materialistic, systematic or historical. Not that a supreme order does not have to reign beyond the line. But "order" does not constitute the original; it remains something founded, just like values. By contrast, your statement at the top of page 272 seems essential to me: "On this side of the line however one is incapable of judging things."

Yet do you not overestimate the contemporary position of the natural sciences in respect of "crossing the line?" Not only are they at a dead end, they are incapable of seeing the dead end by their own means. That traditional philosophy now has nothing to offer, is entirely accurate. But I believe that there is a kind of thinking that is in a position to show what is really taking place when uncertainty has forced itself on physicists.

Since I know how much you appreciate the artisanal work of the author, I allow myself to indicate a triviality.

In the penultimate paragraph of page 252 you establish a correspondence between "intuition (*Anschauung*) and cognition (*Erkenntnis*)" and "image and concept." Because from time immemorial, intuition has been considered to be cognition, yet at this place you want to indicate the non-intuitive, conceptual "con-ceiving" (*Be-greifende*) in contrast with intuition, you should therefore have "judgment" (*Urteil*) there instead of cognition.

But I should merely thank you for the lovely gift, instead of indicating oversights.

Perhaps one day there will be an opportunity for conversation, in which we can go through questions concerning content and style. The two cannot be separated. The question of style is at the same time a mystery of the atelier and of vocation. It does not tolerate public exposition. But it remains for us most necessary and most crucial. Style belongs to the content itself.

Around All-Saints' Day, I was in Messkirch for a few days with my brother and came close to descending upon you in your new house. But time and the opportunities for transportation were then too unfavorable.

Meanwhile, in the midst of the confusion and darkening of the world and exposed to the superpower of a public opinion that distorts and falsifies everything, it seems to me the only thing that remains possible and even adequate is to speak without being heard, simply to respond to the turning of Being in the moments granted. Presumably, it is first necessary to let men know that in such response the voyage into "the immeasurable" begins.

I have yet to thank you for the copy of "Myrdun," that Countess Friderike Podewils brought to the chalet.[14] Among its many beauties, the way you bring this marvelous word to speech suddenly, and only after many pages, is particularly delightful. It awakens the desire to hear the word one day from a Norwegian mouth.

With best wishes,
Yours,
Martin Heidegger

6) Ernst Jünger to Martin Heidegger, 14b
Wilflingen über Riedlingen, 4 January 1951

Dear Herr Heidegger,

I cordially thank you for your lines of 18 December. While it is a shame that you were unable to come to our remote village, hopefully you still send your thoughts. We here are entirely surrounded by dense woods.

Across the Line has interrupted several stories with which I was occupied. I am pleased that these "contributions" have diverted me in this way. The relation to *The Worker* that you evoked is evident. While the writing touches on the other pole—*The Worker* discusses the super-personal/necessary, the *Line*, on the other hand, clarifies the behavior

---

14. *Myrdun. Letters from Norway*, is the account of a voyage of Jünger's from 6 July to 27 August 1935. It was not published until 1943 in a special edition prepared for German soldiers then fighting in Norway. The Countess Friderike von Podewils (1910–2003) was the sister of Count Clemens von Podewils, who served as secretary in Paris to General Heinrich von Stülpnagel, executed for complicity in the plot to assassinate Hitler. Clemens later served as secretary general to the Bavarian Academy of Fine Arts.

of the individual and a new kind of freedom to which it corresponds. I therefore approach the most satisfying part of the task. We Germans are farther than the Americans, who have barely entered into "total mobilization."

I therefore intend to delay a new edition of *The Worker*, in spite of pressure from Klostermann, and to approach certain practical questions from the *Line*, such as the necessary reform of the army. This work nears completion. In its title the word "forest" also appears—today it constitutes a central symbol.

It is probably better to discuss your suggestions *verbally*—in writing they would draw us too far afield. I wish only to anticipate the comment that I attach no particular value to medical terminology. The three other faculties and art offer equivalent levels of approach, and in the final analysis are concepts that become identical—health is freedom, light, the beautiful, divine presence, or even poetry, where the approach takes place as language.

In the morning Friedrich Georg arrives. Clemens Podewils has invited me to Munich for 11 January.[15] Unfortunately, I cannot come, although the subject attracts me. I will drive to Basel on 15 January and remain there for a month. At the beginning of February I return to Freiburg. Will you be there then?

With best wishes for 1951,

Yours,

E. J.

7) Martin Heidegger to Ernst Jünger, Freiburg, 7 January 1951

Dear Herr Jünger,

I thank you for your letter and am pleased with the idea of a conversation in Freiburg. At the beginning of February (only the first is inconvenient) I will be there. You could stay with us. Perhaps you could send us a postcard from Basel when your plans settle.

I quietly hoped to meet you in Munich; it would have been lovely.

---

15. The occasion for the invitation was a performance of Carl Orff's *Antigone*, the libretto for which was Hölderlin's translation of Sophocles' play. To celebrate the event, Podewils organized a series of lectures.

We intend to go on 10 January to Ulm on the rapid. Perhaps your brother could also get a ticket to Riedlingen.

Best wishes and regards,
Yours,
Martin Heidegger

8) Ernst Jünger to Martin Heidegger, 14b Wilflingen über Riedlingen, 16 April 1951

Dear Herr Heidegger,
On the Feast of the Ascension I will be in Freiburg with Herr Klett and Dr. Mohler.[16] If you were there, it would please me to see you. The housing question is taken care of, along with everything else. Please drop me a line.

Yours,
Ernst Jünger

9) Ernst Jünger to Martin Heidegger [postcard], Wilflingen, 23 April 1951

Dear Herr Heidegger,
For the days in Bremen I wish you rest and good success. It would please us to see you in Wilflingen. I have guests until Pentecost, so that a somewhat later day would be preferable.

With best wishes,
Yours,
Ernst Jünger

10) Ernst Jünger, Friedrich Georg Jünger, Ernst Klett, and Armin Mohler to Martin Heidegger [postcard], postmark: Haltingen Kreis Lörrach, 1 May 1951

Dear Herr Heidegger,
At the place mentioned in your favorite poem, we thought of you.[17]

---

16. Armin Mohler (1920–2003), author of *The Conservative Revolution in Germany: 1918–1932*.

17. The poem in question was from a recent publication of Johann Hebel's *Allemannische Gedichte* (1803). Heidegger composed a short essay on Hebel,

Yours,
Ernst Jünger
Kind regards to you and your wife.
Yours,
Friedrich Georg Jünger
I await word of the Hebel first edition—
Yours,
Ernst Klett
Armin Mohler
Haltingen, in "The Stag"

11) Ernst Jünger to Martin Heidegger [postcard], postmark: Basel, 9 February 1952

Dear Herr Heidegger,
   On February 14 I will be in Freiburg and would be very pleased if you had the opportunity to see me. The 13th is equally possible. Please let me know whether the Hotel Oberkirch in Münsterplatz is convenient for you.
   Yours,
   Ernst Jünger

12) Ernst Jünger to Martin Heidegger, Freiburg im Breisgau, 12 February 1952

Dear Herr Heidegger,
   My stay here is unfortunately shorter than I expected. I am only here until tomorrow, and tomorrow noon with Professor Erik Wolf.
   It would be lovely if I could see you for an hour, in the town or in any other place.
   Cordially,
   Yours,
   Ernst Jünger

P.S. I am staying at the Hotel Oberkirch

"Hebel, the Friend of the House" (1957), collected in *Aus der Erfahrung des Denkens*, GA: 13.

13) Martin Heidegger to Ernst Jünger [draft of a letter: after 20 November 1953]

Dear Herr Jünger,

At the time of our last meeting in Munich—during your lecture on "Art in the Age of Technology"—there arose in me the desire that you and Heisenberg and I would enjoy a good hour of conversation.[18] Concerning what, you ask? Concerning what none of us is qualified to discuss alone. The hours for such a conversation cannot be arranged in advance; conversations where the name, the works and the person of the speakers fade away, and where the inexpressible would express itself for them, are perhaps only a dream.

When we exchanged a last greeting from different sides of the street amidst a wasteland of traffic, it seemed to me as if a favorable moment had passed during those days. How many such moments do we let pass unnoticed! In order to catch one or another of them, it is unnecessary to be hasty, but rather to collect them, to consider in retrospect the past possibility, by trying to see whether another granting arrives from it.

14) Martin Heidegger to Ernst Jünger, Freiburg, 15 January 1954

Dear Herr Jünger,

Thank you for the little volume with the excellent Afterword. I congratulate you on your inclusion in the "library." I still think fondly about our visit to Munich and wished once again that a conversation would arise concerning the essential things that move us.

With warmest regards from my wife, and with friendship, I remain Yours,
Martin Heidegger

15) Martin Heidegger to Ernst Jünger, Freiburg im Brelsau, 31 March 1955

Dear Ernst Jünger,

For nearly a year I have delayed writing in homage of your sixtieth

---

18. Werner Heisenberg (1901–1976), author of the "uncertainty principle" in physics, and recipient of the Nobel Prize in 1932 for his creation of quantum mechanics.

birthday. And still I come with personal best wishes on the correct date, only too late.

You however depend the least on precise calculations. You know about other things. That this knowledge in the coming decade of your life is woven into the constitution of the comprehensive work you may have in mind, is my first wish. The second concerns the basic conditions for creativity: health, endurance, friendship, confidence in the original power of the spirit.

Today we are not only solitary and isolated. We are also deprived of the prospect of the secure and constant movement of history, which could immediately promise a later, that is, more original appropriation of the attempted work.

Quite another assurance is necessary for the small number of those who struggle to configure a space adapted for a freedom that not only is suitable for human deeds and gestures, but also, as the foundation of the world, is the free itself, wherein everything appears more inceptively.

In place of simple understandings that only escape into the sameness of a compromise [*ins Gleiche eines Ausgleiches*] and that mask the fecundity of oppositions, it is necessary to enter into the con-frontation [*Aus-einander-setzung*], through which each is brought into its proper character [*Eigenes*] and is recognized therein.

You should be pleased with the attempt at such a con-frontation in the *Festschrift*. Today I follow it with this sign of sincere remembrance.

My wife and I offer you our warmest regards,

Yours,

Martin Heidegger

16) Ernst Jünger to Martin Heidegger, (14b) Wilflingen über Riedlingen, 29 November 1955

Dear Herr Heidegger,

Herr Klostermann, with whom I have spent time in Homburg, sent me your *Essay on the Question of Being*.[19]

---

19. *Zur Seinsfrage*, the title Heidegger gave to a separate publication of the essay *Über "die Linie."*

In that way, I learned that your fine contribution to my *Festschrift* has also appeared in a separate volume. I will read it with attention once again in the new form, keeping in the back of my mind that I could perhaps append something to it—not in the sense of a response, but of a new start, since it is so stimulating. Thus, in the course of the anniversary a chain or a string could result.

With best wishes,

Yours,

Ernst Jünger

P.S. I have now completed a work concerning Rivarol.[20] His maxims are in general crystal clear, although in places a bit orphic, like the following:

Le mouvement entre deux repos est l'image du present entre le passé et l'avenir. Le tisserand qui fait sa toile fait toujours ce qui n'est pas.[21]

This admits of many interpretations. I read it more or less like this:

The present is the motion between the unmoved future and the unmoved past. The weaver weaves his fabric from non-being.

(possibly the translation is: *into* non-being. He "makes" what is not—that can be related to his activity but also to what is made).[22] It does not suffice merely to translate this maxim, but to see it clearly, and there I would be very anxious to know what you, who have reflected so long on time and being, would say about it.

17) Martin Heidegger to Ernst Jünger [postcard], Freiburg, 31 December 1955

Dear Herr Jünger,

Thank you for the postcard. My attempt at an interpretation of Rivarol comes in the next few days.

---

20. Antoine de Rivarol (1753–1801), a reactionary essayist who defended the *ancien régime*. In 1956, Jünger lectured on Rivarol; the lecture was later published in French translation under the title *Rivarol et autres essais* (Bernard Grasset, 1974). For Rivarol's maxims, see his *Maximes et pensées* (A. Silvaire, 1960).

21. Rivarol: 59.

22. "The non-being would then be the action." Note added by Jünger.

With best wishes for the New Year,

Yours,
Martin Heidegger
(The hut in Todtnauberg)²³

18) Martin Heidegger to Ernst Jünger, Freiburg im Bresgau, 1 January 1956

Dear Herr Jünger,

Concerning the text of Rivarol you mentioned, I must offer some reservations before I express myself.

First of all, I am completely unacquainted with Rivarol; as well, I have no edition and therefore no possibility of checking what else Rivarol may have thought and stated about time and motion.

My remarks therefore hang somewhat in mid-air, and are restricted to the text of the maxim you mentioned.

Le <u>*mouvement*</u> *entre deux repos est l'image du present entre le passé et l'avenir. Le tisserand qui* <u>*fait*</u> *sa toile* <u>*fait*</u> *toujours ce qui n'est pas.* "The *motion* between two rests is the image of the present between past and future. The weaver, who *makes* his fabric, always *makes* what is not."

What one notices first of all is the relation between motion-rest (as limit of the moved and its gathering) on the one hand and the temporal on the other. Since Aristotle (*Physics* IV, chapters 10–14) the attention to this relation belongs expressly to the representation of time. But "motion" and "time" are transformed in the process of Western thought into ambiguous expressions, through which the transformed beginnings of Greek thinking always shine. I mention these historical relations which remain obscure in many regards only with respect to the fact that Rivarol is speaking of that issue, *qui n'est pas.*

For Aristotle begins his considerations on time with the question of whether time can be a being, given that it is apparently ἐκ μὴ ὄντων συγκείμενον—it lies before us constituted by non-being, the "not-yet" of the future, the coming, and the "no-longer" of the past. But both

---

23. A marginal note by Martin Heidegger describing the postcard.

these "non-beings" are not nothing (in the sense of *nihil negativum*). If according to Aristotle what properly is (the presencing) in time is the "now," but if this "now" is the transition from the not-yet to the no-longer, then time is determined by κίνησις that is, μεταβολή, change (as change of weather and change of place). Accordingly, the non-beings—the coming and the past—become two different kinds of things that are not at rest. What is present is precisely what is not at rest in the same sense as they are, but instead is the transition.

But what is obscure and at the same time illuminating in Rivarol's maxim lies in the second sentence. The consideration of the weaver, the back-and-forth of the weaver's shuttle, shows that Rivarol sees motion not as an emptying of the future into the past ("time passes"), but as the transition that moves back and forth between two things at rest. However, in so far as past and future no longer belong just as much to "time," what actually is and what remains, what is at rest, seems to "rest" precisely in past and future. Time actually "stands" and does not actually pass; it passes only in as much as it is present, that is, as the transition of passing.

What is decisive in the second sentence I see in the two uses of the word "*fait*" and their ambiguity. This ambiguity comes clear in the question: what does the weaver make? This can mean: 1) what does he produce in the sense of the work of his hands, which work, as issuing from manufacture (pro-duction), is set free into standing for itself and lying at hand; 2) with what is the weaver employed, what is his work, what does he have precisely in hand and under his hand? This second meaning of *faire* and *facere* is historically speaking the first and most authoritative. It means: *poser, placer*, θέσις rather than ποίησις—in fact this, the pro-duction of something from something is in itself already a placing (θέσις) that dis-poses and pro-poses and *trans*-poses. In view of the ambiguous *fait* Rivarol's statement says:

The weaver, who as a weaver of cloth produces and sets out *his* cloth, the cloth woven by him as his work, is in this producing always (*only*) occupied with the back and forth, that is, with the forth to the not-yet, and the back from the "already there," and the reverse. The transition is the presence of non-being. In so far as the weaver is occupied therefore with not-being back and forth, he creates the being, the finished fabric. In the back and forth the present appears. Everything that is present at rest is a stilled back and forth. The vision of the present is yielded not by what is at rest, but by motion. The emphasis of the maxim lies on the first word: *le mouvement*. Customarily we represent what is present as what is unwavering, remaining, and at rest. Rivarol states, however: *Motion* is the vision of the present.

You can easily decide how far this attempt at interpretation stands in harmony with the thought of Rivarol. Such maxims always set our powers of thinking to the test, which is always somehow fruitful.

So I thank you for the reference to this maxim and offer my warmest regards.

Yours,
Martin Heidegger

19) Ernst Jünger to Martin Heidegger, 8 January 1956

Dear Herr Heidegger,

With your analysis of the Rivarol maxim you have not only afforded me an extraordinary joy, but also an extraordinary pleasure.

What was most astonishing to me was the certainty with which you get directly to the kernel, namely Rivarol's representation of time. Since you do not know the author, with this you gave a proof of your powers of exegesis. In effect, time *stands* for Rivarol, as other passages in his work demonstrate. At one time he compares it to the banks of a stream, between which we travel; at another time to a still urn, through which water flows. You have recognized this, like Champollion from a single hieroglyph.

I do not wish to deprive my readers of your explanation in the form of an excerpt, since it also supports my translation, and I would be grateful if you would include the complete text in your shorter writings, since it is on a par with the best of your exegeses.

With heartfelt thanks,
Yours,
E. J.

20) Martin Heidegger to Ernst Jünger [postcard], Freiburg, 22 March 1957

Dear Herr Jünger,

Thank you for your greetings and for your invitation. We would have been glad to come. I will be in Messkirch only later and if possible I will make good on your invitation. Greetings to everyone gathered there.

Cordially,

Yours,

Martin Heidegger

21) Ernst Jünger to Martin Heidegger, 14b
Wilflingen über Riedlingen, 21 November 1957

Dear Herr Heidegger,

Günther Neske sent me *Identity and Difference*.[24] I am on the point of leaving for Paris and will take the book with me. My reading is always deepened by a conversation with Friedrich Georg.

Yesterday I read in *Mercury* Rudolf Pannwitz's comments concerning the three volume Nietzsche collection that Schlechta has brought out.[25] I lack the detailed knowledge to be able to judge the matter, but I feel that something important has happened here—at least, that philosophy is taken as seriously as it must be, and is no longer, in an age where political values dominate or men are simply frightened. I would therefore wish to hear whether this debate has touched you.

Karl Korn sent me a questionaire that he, as I see from his cover note, has also sent you—all difficult questions to which one could respond one way or another. Will you join in?

Cordially, and my regards to your wife,

Yours,

Ernst Jünger

---

24. *Identität und Differenz* (Pfullingen: Verlag Günther Neske, 1957); GA: 11.

25. *Merkur. Deutsche Zeitschrift für europäisches Denken* was founded in 1947 by Hans Paeschke and Joachim Moras. Rudolph Pannwitz (1881–1969) was a German writer, poet, and philosopher whose most famous book, praised by the dramatist Hugo von Hoffmansthal, was *Die Krisis der europäischen Kultur* (*The Crisis of European Culture*) (Verlag Hans Carl Nuenberg, 1917). Karl Schlechta (1904–1985) was a German philosopher and editor of a three-volume edition of Nietzsche's works (*Werke in drei Bänden* [München: Hanser, 1954–1956]). The debate in question concerns the accuracy of the edition, which Schlechta addressed in his book *Der Fall Nietzsche: Aufsätze u. Vorträge* (München: Hanser, 1958).

22) Martin Heidegger to Ernst Jünger, Freiburg im Breisgau, 24 November 1957

Dear Herr Jünger,

Thank you for your letter and I wish you a lovely visit to Paris. Please offer H. S. my greetings.[26] I own the new Nietzsche edition by Schlechta. I had already spoken in detail with Schlechta about this edition during the thirties at the Nietzsche archive. Naturally everything we had in mind at that time could not be realized. But even so I, like you, am pleased that this edition is now present at all. Schlechta is the only one who could still bring it about. Meanwhile, I have no idea what has happened with the archive.

Naturally, I have answered negatively to the *Frankfurter Zeitung*; these sorts of inquiries now multiply on the pages of the big newspapers. I however have nothing at all to do with them.

Hopefully, we will see each other in the coming year; meanwhile, cordial greetings and best wishes to your wife

Yours,

Martin Heidegger

23) Ernst Jünger to Martin Heidegger, 14b Wilflingen über Riedlingen, 29 December 1958

Dear Herr Heidegger,

For the New Year I send you and yours my most cordial wishes. Hopefully we will again meet during it—perhaps in Munich, where my brother will hold a lecture, in January.

In October, in the lovely air of the Engandine, so conducive to concentration, I thought about an undertaking from which technical minds could certainly be excluded, and had the idea for the following game, called Mantrana, the rules of which I enclose for you.[27] Perhaps

---

26. H. S. is probably Hans Speidel (1897–1984), a German general during World War II and the first German NATO commander during the Cold War.

27. Mantrana is a domino game played in two or three dimensions, involving maxims or "mantras" contributed by the players.

you know one or another intelligent partners in your neighborhood, or could contribute a mantra yourself.

With best wishes for 1959

Yours,

Ernst Jünger

24) Ernst Jünger to Martin Heidegger, 2 February 1959

Dear Herr Heidegger,

I am pleased that we saw one another in Munich and already met on the train—hopefully initiating more frequent meetings. Probably I will drive to Rottweil's "fool's leap."[28] I have made arrangements to meet there with Kiesinger.[29] Should you be in Messkirch around this time, I will call on you briefly on the way. For the rest, we expect to see you and your wife soon, in Wilflingen.

In the conversation I had with Heisenberg, he thought that the "peaceful" use of atomic energy is distinct from wartime uses, which are to be held "under control." How long, though? Perhaps as long as the Hague Convention or the penal code obtains.

I am writing you today since General Bouvard has turned to me regarding an affair concerning you.[30] Bouvard, whom I have known for a long time, was Commander of the jet fighters in Lahr, then Commander in Chief of air forces on the west coast of Africa in Dakar, and is today the director of the military academy. I expect even more from him.

He now thinks that a preface by you, for a manuscript he has written concerning modern development that clearly shows the influence of your ideas, would confer on it a particular significance, and he therefore asked me to put the question to you. I of course cannot judge. Perhaps, however, you have among your numerous students one who would be interested in reading this and who could present you with a summary.

---

28. Rottweil, in Baden-Württemberg, is famous for its annual carnival.

29. Kurt Georg Keisinger (1904–1988), affiliated with the Nazi Party, and later a member of the Christian Democratic Party who served as Chancellor of West Germany from 1966 to 1969.

30. Michel Bouvard (1901–1979).

Otherwise, I ask you to return the manuscript to the author: General Bouvard, 73 bis Avenue Niel, Paris 17ᵉ.

I always find it very stimulating in Munich. I am curious about my brother's report concerning Berlin. Again I spent wearying days in Stuttgart, saw Speidel there and a crowd of people, and had to receive a decoration.³¹ As one gets older, he can no longer hide.

With cordial greetings, to your wife, too,

Yours,

E. J.

Hopefully you are entirely restored.

25) Martin Heidegger to Ernst Jünger, Meßkirch, 8 February 1959

Dear Herr Jünger,

Thank you for your letter; I will run through the French text; only first I must make my talk for the Akademie-Jahrbuch publishable.³² This is why I am already leaving tomorrow with my nephew for Freiburg. But in the summer my wife and I will take a walking tour through the old homeland—then we will "descend" upon you.

I regret that there was too little opportunity in Munich for a quiet conversation.

Cordially, from my home to yours,

Yours,

Martin Heidegger

26) Ernst Jünger to Martin Heidegger, 15 February 1959

Dear Herr Heidegger,

Heartfelt thanks for your lines of 8 February. General Bouvard will

---

31. On January 31, 1959, Jünger received the Cross of the Order of Merit of the German Federal Republic.

32. The talk in question is *Der Weg zur Sprache* (*On the Way to Language*), in *Die Sprache. Vortragsreihe München/Berlin*. Fünfte Folge des Jahrbuches *Gestalt und Gedanke*, herausgegeben von der Bayerischen Akademie der Schönen Kunst (München, 1959), 137–70; GA: 12, 227–57.

be pleased to hear from you. It occurs to me that in the spring I will visit some Parisian acquaintances. I will travel by car and in the company of Goslar's city manager, Schneider.[33] What if you joined us? We even have friends in common there. Also, Speidel would be pleased if we sought him out in Fontainbleau.

A cutting from a Hamburg newspaper that contained a scurrilous discussion of the Munich lectures was sent to me. Much labor, care and trouble was spent to prepare such a lecture—then some malicious fool comes along with the preconceived intention to destroy the seeds planted there. One already guesses what motivates it, and "where the shoe pinches him," but is embarrassed to look closer.[34] It pained me above all for the students who had so much invested in the affair. Of course, they could understand little. They however would also probably not have gathered anything more if in your place or my brother's Kant or Schelling had been standing there atop a lectern. I have seen in their very zeal something comforting that honors the lecturers as much as the listeners themselves. There was a good Eros there.

For a moment I felt a desire to state my opinion to these venal beneficiaries of freedom of the press—but it is best to leave them to themselves and to the age, which without fail makes the relative importance of things obvious. One can taste the bitterness over the great success of the lectures all too clearly. Also, they have probably heard some rather unpleasant things. For me, experiences of this sort spoil thoughts of participating again, although I now would have something to say.

I was with Friedrich Georg in Rottweil among the fools and returned Tuesday. Too, there were some diversions in Messkirch, but I drove on, since I knew you were not there.

Please mention me to your wife.

Cordially,

Yours,

E. J.

---

33. Helmut Schneider (1910–1968).

34. The idiom, *wo ihn der Schuh drückt*, "where the shoe pinches him," means to feel the suffering of another.

27) Martin Heidegger to Ernst Jünger, Freiburg, 17 November 1959

Dear Herr Jünger,

I thank you wholeheartedly for your letter. Your approval means more to me than all the rest. One must let poor company leave.

Your travel plan is tempting. Only I still have a new task before me. I promised the President of the Hölderlin Society in Stuttgart to undertake a conference in Munich for this year's meeting ("Hölderlin's Earth and Heaven") in memory of Winkler.[35] For this sort of thing I need considerable time; I therefore ask you to inform me briefly *when* and *for how many* days you plan to be in Paris.

Cordially, and with best wishes,

Yours,

Martin Heidegger

My wife also sends her greetings.

28) Martin Heidegger to Ernst Jünger, Freiburg im Breisgau, Zähringen, Rötebuck 47, 9 May 1959

Dear Herr Jünger,

Herr Schneider, the city manager, wrote to me from Goslar that you would soon leave for France. Sadly, I cannot now go with you, since I am in the middle of working out arrangements for the Hölderlin conference for Munich (the beginning of June).

I wish you a good trip and ask you to send my greetings to Herr Speidel.

All the best to you,

Cordially and best wishes,

Yours,

Martin Heidegger

---

35. Eugen Gottlob Winkler (1912–1936), author of works on Hölderlin, T. T. Lawrence, and Marcel Proust. The conference was to be held on the twentieth anniversary of his suicide. Heidegger's contributions to this conference was published under the title *Erläuterungen zu Hölderlins Dichtung* (*Elucidations of Hölderlin's Poetry*), GA: 4.

29) Ernst Jünger to Martin Heidegger, 30 August 1959

Dear Herr Heidegger,

At the moment of my departure for Sardinia I think of your birthday and send you in advance my heartiest best wishes. I regret that I cannot bring them personally. Herr Mohler will do it for me.

For the beautiful Festschrift I have contributed a mosaic of *At the Wall of Time*. It pleases me that some of my most important thoughts have first been published in this form, for the selection of which I am indebted in particular to Frau Dr. Ruth-Eva Schulz.[36]

Continue to offer us many beautiful things. *Ad multos annos.*

Yours,

Ernst Jünger

30) Ernst Jünger to Martin Heidegger, 14b Wilflingen über Riedlingen, 6 November 1960

Dear Martin Heidegger,

Hopefully you are in good humor and fine form. With me, sadly, things are less cheerful. My wife suffers increasingly.

I have yet to thank you for the beautiful talk that you held in the Cuvilliés Theater on Hölderlin. You unlocked the great texts with care. Please accept the enclosed book from me.[37]

Mircea Eliade and I would be pleased if one day you contributed to the journal *Antaios* that we edit together.[38] I will send you some samples; you will find names that have a good reputation in the world.

The focus of the journal is symbolic explanation; it consists more in a new optic than in new truths. Since all things and relations can be considered in this way, the themes are limitless. A brief exegesis would fit well, like the one you devoted to the jug.[39]

---

36. *An der Zeitmauer* (Stuttgart: Ernst Klett Verlag, 1959). Ruth-Eva Schulz (1918–1995), a student of Hans-Georg Gadamer, who from 1947 to 1950 served as Ernst Bloch's assistant in Leipzig.

37. *Sgraffiti* (Stuttgart: Ernst Klett Verlag, 1960). Jünger dedicated the book to Heidegger.

38. Mircea Eliade (1907–1986), a philosopher and theorist of myth, collaborated with Jünger on the journal *Antaios*, which they directed together until 1971.

39. Jünger is referring to Heidegger's 1950 address, *Das Ding*, in which he illustrated the nature of the "thing" using the example of a jug, GA: 7.

On occasion I have meet with one of your students in Tübingen, Prof. Schulz; we had a good conversation, also with his wife, Ruth-Eva Schulz. Pleasant people, who revere you.

Best wishes,
Yours,
Ernst Jünger

31) Martin Heidegger to Ernst Jünger, 22 November 1960

Dear Herr Jünger,

In these days my thoughts often go out to you, but stop in fear of stirring up your most personal sufferings.[40]

Only at such moments can distance help in inconspicuous ways.

May the mysterious space of deepest solitude—attuned by parting—be in future so imbued for you with *Memory* (*Andenken*), that it always grants anew an as yet unknown nearness, from which you may keep what was taken from you by an unthinkable summons, a summons that awakens profound gratitude.[41]

In remembrance,
Yours,
Martin Heidegger

32) Martin Heidegger to Ernst and Liselotte Jünger, Freiburg, 26 March 1962[42]

Dear Herr Jünger!
Dear Frau Jünger!

We wish you both heartfelt happiness on this beautiful union, which pleases me especially.

Perhaps the opportunity will come once again to visit you from Messkirch.

Cordially, from me and my wife,
Yours,
Martin Heidegger

---

40. On 20 November 1960 Jünger lost his first wife, Gretha von Jeinsen, to a long illness.

41. *Andenken* is the title of a poem by Hölderlin, as well as of an essay of Heidegger's concerning Hölderlin published in *Elucidations* (op. cit.).

42. Jünger was remarried to Liselotte Lohrer on 3 March 1962.

The image on the overleaf is also a souvenir of the visit to the hut, where we spoke about *The Worker*.

33) Ernst and Liselotte Jünger to Martin Heidegger, 26 September 1964

Telegram
Martin Heidegger
Rötebuck 47
Freiburg im Breisgau-Zähringen
On the occasion of today's celebration we think of you and your wife with cordial best wishes.[43] May you, my esteemed Martin Heidegger, light the way for us for a long time still.
Ernst Jünger and wife Liselotte

34) Martin Heidegger to Ernst Jünger, 10 October 1964

Dear Ernst Jünger,
Your wishes and those of your wife are especially gratifying to me. I hope to see you when I am again in Messkirch.
What will you decide about the edition of *The Worker*?
Cordially,
Yours,
Martin Heidegger

The greetings, wishes, and gifts that have been offered me for my final stage on the path of thinking are an encouragement, at the same time signs into the undeserved. How should one give suitable thanks for gratifying signs? Only by questioning continuously: What is called thinking? Is it called:
Thankfulness?
Martin Heidegger

---

43. The celebration is Heidegger's seventy-fifth birthday.

35) Ernst Jünger to Martin Heidegger [postcard], 7941 Wilflingen, 20 October 1964

Dear Martin Heidegger,
We are pleased to hear that you survived your birthday in good order. I expect similar exertions soon.

The Worker meanwhile appeared in its old version as volume IX of my collected works. Hopefully I will one day find the time for a new consideration of this theme.

Please send my regards to your wife.
Cordially,
Yours,
Ernst Jünger and wife Liselotte

In the meantime I will see one of your admirers: Mlle. De Laffoucrière[44]

36) Martin Heidegger to Ernst Jünger, Freiburg im Breisgau, March 1965

Dear, Esteemed Herr Jünger,
That a good spirit, during the next decade, may favor your creations in a style fitting for your age, is my wish for you on this happy day.

One day, these small gifts may please you: the one, concerning Stifter, is dedicated to the poetic, the others will say something to you of the concealed forces of the landscape there.[45]

Cordially, from me and my wife—for you and your wife
Yours,
Martin Heidegger

37) Martin Heidegger to Ernst Jünger, Freiburg im Breisgau, 29 May 1965

Dear, Esteemed Herr Jünger
I have just now received, by express mail and a bit late, the invitation

---

44. Odette Laffoucrière, author of *The Destiny of Thinking and the "Death of God" according to Martin Heidegger* (The Hague: M. Nijhoff, 1968).

45. On the occasion of Jünger's sixty-second birthday, Heidegger sent him first editions of two works: *Adalbert Stifter's Eisgeschichte* (in *Aus der Erfahrung des Denkens* 1910–1976, GA: 1, 185–98 and *On Abraham a Santa Clara*, GA: 16, 598–608).

from the Ministry President Kiesinger to attend a breakfast given in your honor in Stuttgart 1 June.

To my great regret, on that day I am already locked into an out-of-town visit. Not only would I love to be there in your honor, but I would have the particular pleasure to see you again and speak with you.

As a rule though the likes of us must hold to the ancient precept of Lao Tzu:

> "Do not go out the door
> and come to know the world.
> Do not throw open the window
> And see the path of heaven;
> The farther away one goes,
> The less one knows.
> Thus, the wise:
> He makes no journey,
> yet he knows;
> He does not look,
> Yet he offers praise;
> He does not act,
> But he accomplishes."

Best wishes to you and your wife—also from my wife
    Yours,
    Martin Heidegger

38) Ernst Jünger to Martin Heidegger, Djibouti, 8 July 1965, Ship "Hamburg" Hamburg-America Line

Dear Herr Heidegger,

We regret very much that you were not able to be with us in Stuttgart. Hopefully, we will succeed another time. Meanwhile, we are on the way, and have seen oceans, lands, and peoples.

This has given me the chance to reflect on the words of the Chinese sage, which you quoted to me. Could I however alter my temperament and close myself in my room? "Here too there are gods"—and I would at once be tempted to start a journey *autour de ma chambre* like that

French predecessor.[46] It's better then to gain intellectual tranquility and to persist in it, while one's location is changing. That is what I try to do, and will continue to work here on board with the same discipline as in Wilflingen.

Ernst Klett wrote to me at Port Said that he wished to visit you in Freiburg with your student Gerhard Nebel; supposedly this has happened in the meantime. It would be fine if you were to decide on a collected edition. Of course, I have had the experience that an enormous amount of work is connected with it. Perhaps you will manage it with a lighter hand.

With cordial greetings and those of my wife, and the request to send my regards to your wife

Yours,

E. J.

39) Ernst Jünger to Martin Heidegger 7941
Wilflingen über Riedlingen, 1 July 1966

[handwritten addition by Martin Heidegger: "answered 14 July 1966"]

Dear Herr Heidegger,

In view of the underlined passage I ask myself: What do linguistics and metaphysics of language have to do with one another? If there were nothing more to a word than grammar and history we would no longer need either poet or philosopher. Clearly, one shouldn't find this annoying, but just once and for all consider the word "specialist" as a synonym for "idiot."

Cordially,

Yours,

E. J.

[included by Ernst Jünger: a cutting from the *Frankfurter Allgemeinen Zeitung* of 1 July 1966]:

---

46. The expression, "Here too there are gods," is Heraclitus's answer when strangers arrived to visit (*Die Fragmente der Vorsokratiker*, ed. Diels and Kranz [Berlin: Weidmannsche Buchhandlung, 1903], fragment A9). The phrase *autour de ma chambre* is from *Le Voyage autour de ma chambre*, by Xavier de Maistre (1763–1852), an officer in the Russian army and brother of the counterrevolutionary author Joseph de Maistre; the book relates the story of a young officer confined to quarters for forty-two days.

"Pax undergoes a sort of critical revaluation, and students disposed to be all to quick to condemn the unfortunate Chamberlain learn from their professor that the metaphysics of language goes back at least to Fichte, and that even today critical linguists cannot keep Heidegger from gaily pursuing the metaphysics of language. Two hours pass quickly. The students seem anything but passive, although their professor exhausts them through his eminent grasp of the subject and his allusive tactics. One, who apparently just defended his thesis, wishes to know from the sociologist whether languages have a unique character, for example, whether French is a more logical language. Proof: the syntax of the sentence. At this session the answer cannot be found. Even this also reveals that linguistics is an educational speciality [*Bildungsfach*].

We take leave of a professor who practices his teaching as a search for truth along with his students, and who can explain with a smile that there exists no opposition in principle between research and apprenticeship." KARL KORN[47]

[handwritten addition by Ernst Jünger]:
Thus Professor Pollak in the seminar on Romance languages at the University of Frankfurt
FAZ 1 July 1966

40) Martin Heidegger to Ernst Jünger, Meßkirch, 14 July 1966

Dear Herr Jünger,

Thank you for the reference to the paper, which I don't read.

The future, ordered by the development of the computer, belongs to "critical linguistics," semantics, and positivistic analysis of language.

The fact that journalism considers nothing else fits this situation.

What to do? Move on and know that "science" is not capable of deciding about truth.

Cordially, to your and your wife,

Yours,

Martin Heidegger

---

47. Karl Korn (1908–1991). His article titled "For Example, Linguistics: A Visit to the Amphitheater and the Seminar," concerned a course at the University of Frankfurt by Wolfgang Pollack titled "Language and Society in the Study of the Novel." Present at the conference, at Pollack's invitation, was the sociologist Peter Schönbach, from the Institute for Social Research at Frankfurt. During the course

41) Ernst Jünger to Martin Heidegger, 7941
Wilflingen über Riedlingen, 28 July 1966

Dear Herr Heidegger,

In your remarks of 14 July you have once again hit the nail on the head.

The opinions of geologists about granite have changed several times over the last century, while Goethe's texts, insofar as they rest on pure intuition, always stand firm.

Indeed, we live in an age in which theology courts scientific recognition and philosophers are apprenticed to plumbers.

Etymologists know as little about language as Darwinists know about animals. The one strings together words, the other, species, and in the end there remains nothing more than thread, the dry measuring cord. Then they hang themselves from it.

Cordially, from my home to yours,

Yours,

Ernst Jünger

42) Ernst Jünger to Martin Heidegger, 7941
Wilflingen über Riedlingen, 26 August 1966

Dear Herr Heidegger,

I have exchanged correspondence with Dr. Reboul, one of your French disciples.

In addition, a Parisian student, Michel Palmier, who has begun a dissertation on your work, "The Completion of Western Metaphysics according to Nietzsche and Heidegger," wrote to me recently.[48] I showed him your address, but I believe it's quite possible that he has already written to you.

Cordially, and please offer my regards to your wife,

Yours,

Ernst Jünger

---

of the seminar a question arose concerning the writings of the anti-Semitic author Houston Stewart Chamberlain (1855–1927) concerning his idea of an opposition between German and Latin words for "peace."

48. Michel Palmier (1944–1998), a philosopher and art historian.

P. S. Please return Dr. Reboul's letter to me when you have the chance. [Heidegger's copy of the letter included by Ernst Jünger. Handwritten remark of Heidegger: *"Letter to Ernst Jünger* copy"]

Doctor Jean Reboul[49]
30 Chemins de la Barre "old house"
83 Toulon (Var)
10 VIII 66
Sir,

I genuinely feel ashamed opening the last number of *Preuves*, which places the author of *Across the Line* side by side with the slanderous rantings of a "cultured camel" of the College of France, whose principal reason for existing is to direct his fury against the Socrates of Todtnauberg.[50]

(As for the picture, grotesque at many points, which he gives of Hölderlin, it is really less serious, the victim being beyond reach.

Eternity finally changes him into himself . . .)[51]

To me, reading "At the Wall of Time" followed by "The Question Concerning Technology" is so brilliant an image of wisdom and of ἀλέθεια that it seems that each of you must suffer from insults cast at the other.

This Frenchman, at least, apologizes for it.

The friends of Martin Heidegger are your friends, attentive and thankful; and I am yours since "Gardens and Paths"[52]

(When will there be a good translation of *The Worker*?)

Respectfully,

Signed, Jean Reboul

---

49. Dr. Jean Reboul, an ophthalmologist, was interested in the psychoanalytic works of Jacques Lacan. Together with Jacques Taminiaux, he translated Heidegger's *What Is a Thing?* (Paris: Gallimard, 1971).

50. The reference is to Robert Minder (1902–1980), a professor at the College of France, whose article, "Hölderlin chez les Allemands" included a blunt attack on Heidegger's wartime politics (*Preuves*, number 186–87, August–September 1966: 23–24). To Minder, Heidegger's "political deception" sought "shelter in a philosophical poetics" used to justify his unconditional support of Hitler.

51. This is the first verse of Stephane Mallarmé's poem "The Tomb of Edgar Allan Poe" (*Le Tombeau d'Edgar Allan Poe*).

52. Ernst Jünger's Paris diary, *Gärten und Straßen* (Berlin: Mittler, 1942).

43) Martin Heidegger to Ernst Jünger, Freiburg im Breisgau, 27 August 1966

Dear Herr Jünger,

Thank you for passing on the letter from the French doctor. Sadly, your response is absent. I include a carbon copy of your letter to me.

I have heard of the agitations of the gentleman of the College of France, but I have no further knowledge of them. The person in question has, for a few years now, arranged for Wiesengrund-Adorno to come to the College of France, in order to rail against me.[53]

The student whose name you mentioned has still not made himself known.

Cordially, from my home to yours,

Yours,

Martin Heidegger

2 pieces attached

P.S. I have allowed myself to recopy the letter in French; I will take it to Provence, where I've been invited by René Char.[54]

44) Ernst Jünger to Martin Heidegger, 29 August 1966

Dear Herr Heidegger,

Please forgive my absent-mindedness, forgetting to include my reply to Dr. Reboul. Keep it!

Cordially,

Yours

Ernst Jünger

[included by Ernst Jünger]:

---

53. Theodor W. Adorno (1903–1969), a German philosopher and leading member of the Frankfurt School of critical theory. His essay of 1964, *The Jargon of Authenticity* (*Jargon der Eigentlichkeit: Zur deutschen Ideologie*, vol. 4, *Gesammelte Schriften*) (Frankfurt am Main: Suhrkamp, 1973) was an attack on Heidegger's language of authenticity and notions of the self.

54. René Char (1907–1988), French poet.

26 August 1966

Dear Monsieur Doctor Reboul,

I was not informed that an attack against Martin Heidegger had been published in the same number of *Preuves* as my study of Alfred Kubin. Thank you for pointing it out to me.

For my part, I value Martin Heidegger not only for his work, but also because he has exposed himself politically, while it would have cost much less not to do so. Can one reproach him if the political powers have disappointed his confidence in them? To you, as a psychoanalyst, one need not indicate what is hidden behind the denigration of a superior mind.

At least this: that somewhere somehow there is thinking that still merits the name, which cannot be entirely hidden. Your letter confirms this for me.

Cordially,

Yours,

E. J.

45) Ernst Jünger to Martin Heidegger, 18 September 1967

Dear Herr Heidegger,

You will guess that my remarks in the second paragraph concern a common "friend" of ours.[55] Perhaps it is worthwhile to consider the matter closed, that such machinations at least have been noted. They are indeed transparent.

Hopefully you and yours are in good health,

Cordially,

Ernst Jünger

[included by Ernst Jünger]:

18 September 1967

To the Schopenhauer Society

In Frankfurt am Main

My heartiest thanks for your letter of 13 September, and for the

---

55. The friend is Karl Jaspers; see letter 52.

attachments, which I will study at leisure. Arthur Schopenhauer counts among the minds through whose work I have learned to think. I continually return to him, and at this moment, lying in bed with the flu, I occupy myself with reading the third volume of *The World as Will and Representation*.

You know better than I the attempt underway to devalue this classical thinker. Yet his star will still shine, when the false lights of our fashionable philosophers are long extinguished. *Post nubila Phoenix*—they reach his level neither rationally nor metaphysically, not to mention ethically.[56]

Cordially,

E. J.

46) Ernst Jünger to Martin Heidegger, 7941
Wilflingen über Riedlingen, 27 November 1967

Dear Herr Heidegger,

I would like to offer you my thanks today for the dedication of *Wegmarken*, although I have only read half of it.[57] I wish in this grey November to go to Paris for one or two weeks.

Your texts are difficult and barely translatable; I am still always astonished by the influence they exercise over French intellectuals. It must therefore occur by a sort of osmosis, or else the reader follows some connection that exists beneath the level of language.

The objections of etymologists against your style of writing are not valid, since you penetrate beneath the historical constructs of language. The same counts for logic and for experience in general. It is reduced to a few enormous steps.

This kind of grounding is more fruitful than attempts to build up language where it has long been in decline. In this respect you correctly see Hölderlin as a singular phenomenon. His language, too, is to be fathomed, not "understood."

---

56. "After clouds, a phoenix." Jünger has altered a Latin proverb that should read: "post nubile, Phoebus"—"after clouds, sun."

57. See GA: 9. Heidegger's dedication reads: "To Ernst Jünger, cordially, Martin Heidegger."

> "We are a sign, uninterpreted,
> —and have nearly
> lost our tongue in a strange land."[58]

This shadows your situating of language as "the house of Being." The formula is often cited, but rarely in the sense of the wordless and nameless Mnemosyne, who at the same time indicates certainty and loss.

It is in the nature of things that what is exciting, the genuine daring of your way of thinking, is more intuited than specified. One day this will contribute to the fame not only of our country but also of our age. It complements their strenuous efforts on behalf of organization and management.

I'm pleased that your judgment about *The Worker* remains unchanged. Nothing in the spirit of the times has changed your judgment, just as that time it was not forced by it. The book remained in essence unnoticed and covered over or veiled by the mere course of events, although its diagnoses and prognoses are confirmed daily. At least, it is a better fate than to enjoy world attention, while things take a completely different course. So it is with Marx—the facts contradict the conception, thoughts contradict actions. Materially, it already came to an end with the steam engine; meanwhile, with electricity and atomic technology, two further giant strides have occurred. The discrepancy does not decrease the progress of events; but most likely the consciousness of estrangement and desolation increases.

I have been occupied with the "clearing of Being." In the absolute, probably, a loss, but only in this way can the original light split into faculties—into good and evil, certainty and doubt. Ought one admit in accordance with your conception that a dilution occurs here, just as in homeopathy the potentization of a substance simultaneously dissolves it, diminishes it, and makes it more efficient?

A small note for a new edition, p. 8, paragraph 3, "Being so inclined"—a "to us" seems to have been dropped.

Perhaps you have already heard that I recently met your son in Bonn. I thought about the day years ago that we spent together in Todtnauberg, when he returned from captivity in Russia.[59]

---

58. The first verse of Hölderlin's poem, "Mnemosyne." Jünger has omitted part of the second line, "Schmerzlos sind wir" ("Painless we are").

59. Hermann Heidegger (born 1920) served as an infantry officer and was captured by the Soviet army in 1945.

My wife also sends her greetings.
Cordially,
Yours,
Ernst Jünger

47) Ernst Jünger to Martin Heidegger, 7941 Wilflingen über Riedlingen, 15 August 1968

Dear Herr Heidegger,
   Returning from Iceland, I found the invitation to the celebration in Amriswil in the mail.[60] It pleases me particularly to read that you too will participate in it. My brother is thoroughly familiar with your work and its significance, with which he has occupied himself for a decade.
   Between brothers self-praise is difficult—I would probably be content with a short exposition of the current state of intellectual existence and its difficulties, without polemic and lasting no longer than twenty minutes.
   As I wrote to you a while before, the "clearing of Being" has particularly occupied me, and in connection with the planned text, I would like to learn in a sentence whether one can "step out" into this clearing.* Or do I have too plastic a representation of a rather atmospheric process? The reader often spins off in directions that the author did not intend.
   With cordial greetings,
   Ernst Jünger

[handwritten remark of Martin Heidegger]
*) We are always already standing *in* it—without having until today properly experienced it as such and sufficiently thought it.

48) Martin Heidegger to Ernst Jünger, Freiburg im Breisgau-Zähringen, Rötebuck 47, 19 August 1968

Dear Herr Jünger,
   Thank you for your letter. I answer at once, and am pleased to see you again on so beautiful an occasion.

---

60. The invitation was to celebrate Friedrich Georg Jünger's seventieth birthday.

We need not first "step out" into the clearing, since we always already stand in it. This in-standing determines ex-istence. But the clearing was up to now not properly thought. The first echo however resounds in Ἀ-λήθεια, providing that we think this in the Greek sense, instead of misinterpreting it through the traditional concept of truth.

I am sending you the French text of a lecture from the year 1964; I have not read it myself in Paris. The German text has not yet appeared, I do not even have it on hand. I request the return in due course of the attached personal copy.[61]

I still owe you my heartfelt thanks for the beautiful "Subtle Hunts."[62] In my judgment it is, next to *The Worker*, the best, most successful book you have written.

My contribution to the celebration in Amriswil consists in some remarks about a barely noticed text of Hölderlin concerning the poet, recently published.[63] But I ask you not to divulge this yet, to preserve the element of surprise.

Cordially, and my regards to your wife

Yours,

Martin Heidegger

49) Ernst Jünger to Martin Heidegger, 7941
Wilflingen über Riedlingen, 4 September 1968

Dear Herr Heidegger,

I am sending back your piece from the archives with deepest thanks. I will continue to occupy myself with the "clearing." In my reading, it further struck me how on the one hand the translation into French accentuates such texts, and on the other hand makes them sterile and uniform. That is a gain and a loss; in every elucidation, clarification is

---

61. The reference is to "La fin de la philosophie et la tâche de la pensée" ("The End of Philosophy and the Task of Thinking"), in *Kierkegaard vivant* (Paris: UNESCO, 1966). The German text, "Das Ende der Philosophie und die Aufgabe des Denkens," appeared originally in *Zur Sache des Denkens* (Tübingen, 1969), GA: 14.

62. *Subtile Jagden*, Stuttgart, 1967 (*Sämtliche Werke*, vol. 10, Klett-Cotta, 1998).

63. See Heidegger's *Erläuterungen*, op.cit.

bound up with diminishment. The "both-and" is transposed into an "either-or."

I wish also to thank you for *Time and Being*, your important gift on the occasion of the successful celebration at Amriswil. It has accompanied me on the trip home, together with the new poems of Friedrich Georg. Here as there one is happy with the almost indiscernible development of the perspective opening within.

> "Let go all fear! It is certain.
> So tender, Anemone, is your trust."[64]

With cordial greetings, to your wife as well,
Yours,
Ernst Jünger

50) Ernst Jünger to Martin Heidegger, 7941 Wilflingen über Riedlingen, 7 November 1968

Dear Herr Heidegger,

The book by Jean-Michel Palmier will be coming to you.[65] I do not know what judgment you have formed of it; in these quarrels one often feels as if one lived on the moon.

It seems to me that the still remarkably young author merits encouragement; I therefore wrote him the attached letter.

In the hope that you and your wife are in good health,
I remain, cordially,
Yours,
Ernst Jünger

[included by Ernst Jünger]
Ernst Jünger

4 November 1968

Dear Herr Palmier,

Receive my heartfelt thanks for kindly sending *The Political Writings of Heidegger*. Martin Heidegger will also have been pleased with your

---

64. Friedrich Georg Jünger, *Es pocht an der Tur* (Frankfurt am Main: Klostermann, 1968), 71.

65. Jean-Michel Palmier, *Les Écrits politiques de Heidegger* (Paris: L'Herne, 1968).

work. I met him in September in Amriswil, where Swiss friends gave a celebration in honor of my brother Friedrich Georg's seventieth birthday.

The controversies regarding this philosopher are a perfect example of the incompatibility between political interests and intellectual capacities. Admittedly, one must consider that there are only a few elephants, but many elephant lice. They rush onto the monster on which they live, and yet find only the food for which they are adapted.

You are careful to unlock for your countrymen the fund of words that hides beneath the difference between languages. That is not easy, and I myself often wonder about the effect that Heidegger's terminology, difficult even for us Germans, has found in France. His thinking leads back resolutely to the word and to language.

"*La figure du travailleur.*" Here it must be explained: "figure" is first of all not "phenomenon" (*Erscheinung*), it is a contouring within the phenomenal world. "*Travail*" goes back to the Latin "tripalium," an instrument of torture. "Arbeit" (work) comes from the Gothic "arpeo," which means inheritance.

One can locate the whole of Marxism in the form of the worker, but not the reverse. Machine technology is the garment of the worker, even his global language.

As I gather from the prospectus, you are still astonishingly young. That is good. We therefore must hope that you will occupy yourself often, and fundamentally, with this theme that you already touched so fortunately with your first attempt.

In the meantime, I return over and over again to the worker. I add for you a small list of titles, as far as they have appeared in book form.

The detail first becomes fruitful when it is grouped around a limited center, from which social, political, technical, economic developments stem.

Best wishes,

Yours,

E. J.

51) Martin Heidegger to Ernst Jünger, Freiburg im Breisgau, 20 November 1968

Dear Herr Jünger,

Thank you for your letter and for the copy of your encouragement to Jean-Michel Palmier.

I have only just begun to read his book. It certainly represents a great deal of work and the efforts at "objectivity" are clear. The author however has a greater gift for journalism than for thinking. He has already written too much for his age. But perhaps he can learn to learn. I do not appreciate this sort of literature—whether for or against or in-between. Nevertheless, it still runs wild, and meets a need arising from boredom.

Cordially, from home to home,
Yours,
Martin Heidegger

52) Ernst Jünger to Martin Heidegger, 7941
Wilflingen über Riedlingen, 10 January 1969

Dear Herr Heidegger,

I was pleased by Leonhard Fischer's thoughts on your 79th birthday.[66] Brief, precise, appropriate to the significance of the subject, not once letting itself be polemical. One can agree with every statement—up to the political "straying"; before the weight of those fateful hours is recognized, many years yet must pass, and much in the world must change.

I was unaware that you, as I believe one could conclude from the essay, had a negative relation to Schopenhauer. My answer to the Schopenhauer Society, a copy of which I sent you, arose from a fresh impression of a remark of Jaspers promulgated in the press: Schopenhauer was not the intellectual representative of the century, but rather Heinrich Heine! I noted that to be one of the low points of German philosophy, as was, in his age, Bäumler's question to Spengler: hadn't he read the newspapers?[67] In the political arena this corresponds to a German city's bestowing a peace prize on Churchill.

That should not distract me; the type is poorly represented since

---

66. Leonhard Fischer (1930–2008), a philosopher whose essay, "For the 79th Birthday of Martin Heidegger" was published in the journal *Das Katherineum* (n.61, 1968).

67. Alfred Bäumler (1887–1968), a German philosopher who used Nietzsche's thought to justify National Socialism. In his Parisian Journal, in an entry dated 7 October 1942, Jünger expressed indignation at Bäumler's criticism of Spengler.

1888.[68] In any case, Fischer's explanations show that there is always something to think about.

Best wishes,

Yours,

Ernst Jünger

53) Martin Heidegger to Ernst Jünger, Freiburg im Breisgau, Rötebuck 47, 2 February 1969

Dear Herr Jünger,

I have yet to thank you for your letter of 10 Jan.; I am not at all acquainted with Leonhard Fischer, even less with his article. I would be grateful if you would send it to me sometime.

Your judgment of my relationship to Schopenhauer is correct, only I would not label it so crassly as "negative"; I have consistently recognized Schopenhauer's significance for the philosophy of the 19th century. To the remark of Jaspers, one can only say: "I don't know what it ought to mean"—[69]

Best wishes and greetings to your and your wife,

Yours,

Martin Heidegger

54) Ernst Jünger to Martin Heidegger, 7941 Wilflingen, 5 February 1969

Dear Herr Heidegger,

Great thanks for your lines. I have asked Herr Fischer to send you a copy of his essay. The *laudatio* also pleased Gerhard Nebel, who visited me here recently.

Cordially,

Yours,

Ernst Jünger

---

68. 1889 was the year of Nietzsche's madness, to which Jünger may be alluding here.

69. The first verse to Heine's poem, "Lorelei," from *Buch der Lieder* (*Book of Songs*) in *Historisch-kritische Gesamtausgabe der Werke*, Band I, ed. Manfred Windfuhr (Hamburg: Hoffmann und Campe, 1975), 206–09.

55) Ernst Jünger to Elfride Heidegger, 7941 Wilflingen, 30 May 1969

My very dear Frau Heidegger,

Your husband's 80th birthday approaches, and I take it that, as usual, the major burden rests with you.

The following, therefore, in confidence: I do not know if I will be in Germany on that day. In any case, I have prepared a short writing that should be dedicated in print to your husband and be presented at the birthday.[70] I did something similar twenty years ago with *Across the Line*. This text however is not appearing with Klostermann, but as a modest, independent homage. Should I be traveling, my brother or a third party will present it, in the event you hold an open house. If not, there is always the mail. I take it that the one celebrating will be glad when he has the day behind him.

For your amusement and for you to keep I include a short correspondence that I had with the mayor of my hometown, Rehburg. The citizens there had the idea to christen a new school after me, which however was opposed by the government of Lower-Saxony. I was rather relieved about that, because such an honor mostly occasions new terms of abuse. Best that I should put a clause in my will in which I refuse to tolerate it posthumously—I already dread the people "that then will come."

We often have the same guests, recently again the sympathetic M. Palmier. I am sorry that you have not received Vintila Horia; he is particularly worthy of it.[71]

Cordially, and with best wishes,

Yours,

E. J.

56) Elfride Heidegger to Ernst Jünger, 15 June 1969

Dear Herr Jünger,

Thank you for your letter. My husband will regret that you cannot

---

70. *Federbälle* (*Shuttlecocks*), originally published in a limited edition by Wege und Gestalten (Biberach an der Riss, 1969).

71. The Romanian novelist Vintila Horia (1915–1992) was banned from receiving the Prix Goncourt in 1960 for his novel *God is Born in Exile*, an imag-

take part in the birthday celebration in Amriswil. This Swiss "world village" understands particularly well how to organize a celebration that burdens no one. An 80th birthday though is a punishment from God; but how does one escape it?

I have said nothing to my husband about your intended gift; it will please him—more than other presents. The mayor of his hometown Messkirch told me in confidence that he would name a new Gymnasium to be built there the "Martin Heidegger Gymnasium."[72] I hope that the authorities in Stuttgart say no, just like those in Hanover.

Cordially, to your and your wife,

Yours,

Elfride Heidegger

57) Ernst Jünger to Martin Heidegger [undated]

Dear, honored Martin Heidegger,

Shuttlecocks: on the occasion of your 80th birthday I have selected a series of notes under this title that have occurred on the margins of my work and reading, corrections, correspondences, and conversations. They stem from a stock of mostly critical and self-critical remarks about language and style.

If a red thread runs through these observations that are tied to fleeting occasions, it is the pleasant surprise of the Lower Saxon who feels comfortable with the Alemannic linguistic region and is familiar there.[73] Perhaps you too, from the other side, can share a bit in this comfort; it would please me.

Cordial best wishes,

Ernst Jünger

---

inary journal of the Latin poet Ovid, for his membership in the "Iron Guard," a Romanian fascist group, during World War II.

72. The Gymnasium was finally dedicated in 1973 under the name "Messkirch Gymnasium."

73. Alemannic is a group of Upper German dialects, spoken in parts of Germany, Switzerland, Austria, Liechtenstein, and Alsace. Swabian is an alemannic dialect spoken in the region of Heidegger's childhood. The following letters discuss this dialect.

58) Martin Heidegger to Ernst Jünger, Freiburg in Breisgau, 7 November 1969

Dear, honored Ernst Jünger,

The *Shuttlecocks*, with the dedication rife with memories, are a special gift to me. What remains unsaid in it touches the innermost regions of my efforts at thinking.

The little volume belongs at the worktable of every serious writer. It substitutes for the "philosophies of language" now proliferating.

But who attends anymore to the mysterious speaking of language to which one corresponds less and less, to the lawfulness of its play?

If I hearken back to my youth, to the Upper Swabian language of my homeland that lies so near your current residence, then I recognize with horror how since then the language has become flat and is dying out. Furthermore: one is "embarrassed" today still to speak in dialect and completely forgets that the language of the mother is—i.e., was, the mother of language.

In conversation with old people, who are becoming rare, the language is still to be heard. My wish is that you may still hear much that is surprising, note it and preserve it—but at the same time encounter a peculiar self-satisfaction, as expressed in the following Swabian proverb: "Wa(s) goht mi mei saudomms Gschwätz vu geschtert ä. . . ."

Two examples for your careful grammatical consideration: after 1945 "a cousin of mine" insisted on saying: "i bi nie kein Nazi gsei."

At a eulogy the speaker said of the deceased: "Sei Vatter starb mit fünf Johr."[74]

Dear honored Ernst Jünger! I thank you heartily for your gift.

Greetings and best wishes to you, from home to home,

Yours,

Martin Heidegger

---

74. Compare to the standard German: "Was geht mich mein Geschwätz von gestern an" ("What do I care about what I said yesterday"). The second expression: "Ich bin nie ein Nazi gewesen" ("I was never a Nazi"). The third expression: "Sein Vater starb fünf Jahren" ("His father died five years ago"). It is interesting to note that in the second sentence, the Swabian dialect uses a double negative ("nie keine); hence, Heidegger's reference to grammar, and not just semantics.

On the attached sheet I note some of what just occurred to me while reading "Shuttlecocks."

Attachment

p. 11: "*Zwiesel*"—is a more common name for the tree from whose basic trunk two main trunks grow.

p. 20 The *question*: "Kennte mr morge it (nicht) dresche?"—is also more common in the uplands.[75]

p. 25 "D' Butte" for us is a feminine noun. I still see my father with a double use for (i.e., while carrying) the "tub":

as a cellarman, "drawing off" the wine from large barrels into small kegs (so it was done in the cellars of the Messkirch castle, where the *Zimmer Chronicle* was written);[76]

as sexton, filling the "fonts" with fresh water for sprinkling on the morning of Easter Saturday.

p. 25 regarding "Bletz," a classical passage from Johannes Peter Hebel's dialogue "The Transitory," around the conclusion of the first answer of Aetti: "es chömme Chindes-Chind/ und pletze dra" (am "Hus") "pletze" = flicken ("that the son comes to the son to tinker there" (in the house); pletze = tinker).[77]

p. 25 "Glufe" = pins. In our early childhood, our mother had the habit of saying that when we planned something unseemly, "Wenn du des machscht, kumscht ufs Glufehüfele" (where the poor souls sit in Purgatory and must atone).[78]

p. 26 regarding "zentralst": "the best wine": "der primaschte Wei"

p. 29 "Lichtung" does not belong to "Licht" ("light") but to "leicht" [light, not heavy]; "die Anker lichten" ["raise anchors"], they are made loose, free; the free place in the woods; it is also free in the darkness—light.

---

75. In standard German, "Hätte mir morgen wasche könne" ("Can you wash it for me tomorrow?")

76. The chronicle of Froben Christoph von Zimmer (1519–1566), who resided in Messkirch.

77. Johann Peter Hebel (1760–1826), a German author celebrated for a collection of Alemannic poems; see his *Sämmtliche Werke* (Carlsruhe: Müller'-schen Hofbuchhandlung, 1838), Band I. Heidegger's essay on Hebel, "Hebel, der Hausfreund" ("Hebel, The Friend of the Family"), is in GA: 13.

78. "If you do this, you'll sit on a heap of pins."

59) Ernst Jünger to Martin Heidegger, 7941
Wiflingen, über Riedlingen, 26 December 1969

Dear, Honored Martin Heidegger,

I must again offer you my heartfelt thanks before St. Sylvester's Day for enriching my library. Your words on my Swabian excursus please me no less. On the occasion of *Shuttlecocks* there begins to develop a back-and-forth that brings unexpected turns. I therefore hope that I can dedicate a second volume to you at a fitting opportunity.

Particularly fruitful for me was your point of view on *Lichtungen*. I must still respond to this subject in detail, as well as to the language of the sexton and the cellarman. For the time being, I am compelled to say that your short writing "Art and Space" has spoken deeply to me.[79] Hopefully you will come to further excavate the seam that you have only begun to mine.

I think the principal effect of these investigations is to escape the "crushing" orientations of critical epistemology—not in the sense that these would be annulled, but rather, that they would be placed in the history of thinking. In this way a door lifted off its hinges does not lose its sense, but only its actual or even epochal function.

You advance from the word to the material. In this connection, the sense of the word *aufgeräumt* ["expansive"] came to me. The relation between mood and space is noteworthy; other languages stress light, cheerful, festive resonances. "*In high spirits, festivus, allegro, éveillé.*" The prefix *auf* serves to intensify: *aufgeheitert, aufgemuntert, aufgeweckt* ["enlivened," "elevated," "reveling"].

How then is the spatial intensified by *Aufräumen* [cleaning out, putting in order]? Probably in such a way that the inessential things are removed *en masse*, that they no longer interfere. Then the essence comes forth. In this way one clears away the tables and chairs from a dancehall. It is now brighter, more free, lighter—cheerfulness is without reason: we are cleared up.

By clearing up, one gains the *lumen* from *volumen*, the bright expanse from the massive form. From difficulty comes ease; volume goes back to *volvo*, *lumen* to *luceo*.

The text will greatly occupy me.

---

79. GA:13, 203–10.

For the time being, I wish, also in the name of my wife, a happy, peaceful and fulfilling New Year to you and yours.

Yours,

Ernst Jünger

P. S. We still have here in Wilflingen, as concerns language, a very fine "patrimony." It therefore does not seem difficult to me to follow your suggestion and to note what I hear "over the fence."

From the farmers, whose electrical bills are always higher and higher, I have picked up a word that has almost disappeared from use. They say: "Das Geld beschießt nimmer" ["There's never enough money"— literally, "the money never fires"].

I was in Munich a short while ago and during my absence the mailman, having had worries, felt that a great weight had fallen from his chest, so that, as we in Hanover say, "it went boom." He asked: "Hent se's net bockle here z'Minka?" ["Could you hear the noise in Munich?"]

60) Elfride and Martin Heidegger to Liselotte Jünger, Freiburg im Breisgau/Zähringen, Rötebuck 47, 3 March 1970

Dear Frau Jünger,

It is quite kind of you to invite us to the approaching celebration. We cordially thank you for it. Sadly, it is not possible for us to come, since over Easter our children and grandchildren, who have to take this trip during the holidays, are coming to visit us from north Germany. We regret very much not being able to come, since you have indeed written about an unusually tempting program. So it only remains to us to thank you and to wish that you both are well and the celebration goes joyfully.

My husband wants to be able to leave a small present that he will send to your address with the request to lay it on the birthday table.[80]

With cordial wishes and greetings we are

Yours,

Elfride and Martin Heidegger

---

80. Heidegger sent Jünger the original manuscript of the essay "Adalbert Stifter's *Ice Story*," GA: 13.

61) Ernst Jünger to Martin Heidegger [Pentecost 1970]

"Time and its many forms begins to turn toward a new look, which divines substance not only behind the masks, but in the masks themselves. The flourishing of morphology of culture at the beginning of the century indicates as much. This discovery, layer by layer, each of which fascinates but in the last analysis fails to satisfy, as if one kept seeking the Troy of the poet under the rubble of newly destroyed cities, is one of our greatest experiences.

Refinements of materialism must precede. Not all who seek life here make a find. The sarcophagus with its covering of stone, wood and metal only hides a mummy. Sill there is more there, as the scarab reveals. When he moves his wings, everything comes to life, even the hardest stone."

From *Approaches*,
The manuscript of which I completed today.[81]
+

With cordial thanks for all good wishes and gifts on 29 March 1970
Wilflingen, Pentecost 1970   Ernst Jünger
Herr Professor
Martin Heidegger
7800 Freiburg-Zähringen
Rötebuck 47
[handwritten remark of Ernst Jünger]
Dear honored friend, your manuscript stole the show! I will write about it later. On Wednesday we travel to the Grand Canary, to recover from the birthday.

Cordial greetings, from my wife, too

62) Ernst Jünger to Martin Heidegger, 7941 Wiflingen, über Riedlingen, 27 July 1970

Dear, Honored Martin Heidegger,
I only got around today to sending you your copy of *Ad Hoc*, an

---

81. *Annäherungen: Drogen und Rausch* (*Approaches: Drugs and Noise*) (Stuttgart: Ernst Klett, 1970).

edition that includes, among other things, my contribution to the *Fest-schrift* on the occasion of your eightieth birthday.[82] The annoyances that accompanied my own birthday delayed me terribly. In the interim we recovered on the Grand Canary, but it was already quite hot there.

As I hear, the celebration also had consequences for your health that are probably by now improved. Todtnauberg must have been salutary for that.

Your manuscript has given me particular pleasure.[83] The sight of your handwriting always prepares me for new satisfactions. Besides, it makes me think about your agreement with Marbach—I am allowed to mention it, since it has been spoken about in a wider circle.[84] I find myself in a comparable situation—on the one hand I must reflect on the security of my archives, in which, in the course of half a century, an enormous collection of letters, manuscripts, books have accumulated; on the other hand it would not be awful for me if I finally for once built a house. The matter is not urgent. But it would be good if you or your wife would one day mention whether it generally pays to consider it. *Quieta non movere*, that is mostly proven true.[85] Today, construction mainly brings annoyance; besides, I enjoy living in houses that go back at least two centuries, in which substance has accumulated.

With cordial greetings and best wishes,

Yours,

Ernst Jünger

63) Ernst Jünger to Martin Heidegger [postcard], 7941 Wiflingen, über Riedlingen, 15 December 1970

Dear, honored Martin Heidegger,

Heartfelt thanks for *Phenomenology and Theology*.[86] I return from

---

82. *Ad Hoc* (Stuttgart: Ernst Klett, 1970). It included his essay, *Federbälle*.

83. The manuscript was Heidegger's essay, "Adalbert Stifters *Eisgeschichte*."

84. In December, 1969 Heidegger sold the manuscript of *Being and Time* along with those of his writings published up to that date to the German Literature Archive of Marbach, in order to finance completion of his house.

85. "Be still and do not move."

86. GA: 9.

Paris, having spoken a great deal with Palmier and several others about your work.

Cordial wishes to you and yours for 1971.

Yours,

Ernst Jünger

64) Ernst Jünger to Martin Heidegger [postcard]
7941 Wiflingen, über Riedlingen, 12 March 1972

Dear, honored Martin Heidegger,

After not hearing from you for a long time, *Schelling's Treatise . . .* came this day. However provisional, my heartfelt thanks![87]

With best wishes,

Yours,

Ernst Jünger

65) Ernst Jünger to Martin Heidegger, 7941
Wiflingen, über Riedlingen, 24 November 1972

Dear, Honored Martin Heidegger,

I found your name as well on the list of invitees for the 2 December in Amriswil. That awoke in me the hope to see you again in that pleasant place.

On this occasion I wish to signal my embarrassment over a citation. I remembered in the course of my work a central place in which you spoke of "Nothing." It always resonates when you speak about Being, yet this paragraph is particularly dense. It would be wonderful if you would help me out. Unfortunately, it is often this way for me, when I am questioned about my own citations I no longer remember the place, or even the statement itself.

With cordial greetings, to your wife, too, and best wishes,

Yours,

Ernst Jünger

---

87. Heidegger, *Schellings Abhandlung. Über das Wesen der menschlichen Freiheit (1809)* [*Schelling's Treatise. On the essence of human freedom, 1809*], ed. Hildegard Feick (Tübingen, 1971). Reprinted in GA: 42 under the title *Schelling: Vom Wesen der menschlichen Freiheit (1809)*. See also the translation, *Schelling's Treatise on the Essence of Human Freedom*, trans. Joan Stambaugh (Athens: Ohio University Press, 1985).

66) Ernst Jünger to Martin Heidegger 941
Wiflingen, über Riedlingen, 28 November 1972

Dear, Honored Martin Heidegger,

You answered my question unexpectedly soon—much thanks! That has been useful to me.

Once again I am occupied with additional notes on *Across the Line*. On this occasion, I am taken up with Arabic numerals, and in particular with the zero, as the *non ulla res* [no thing], and the intellectual difficulties tied up with this sign. I approvingly quoted the statement of Karl Menninger on his *Cultural History of Number*:

"The zero is a sign that must *exist* [*dasein*] in order to express that *nothing* is there." In this respect, recollections of your works arise spontaneously.

It is a shame that you will not come to Amriswil, but also understandable. You will surely be thought of there, since you are tied in a particular way to the *genius loci* [the genius of the place], and hopefully too the *Heidegger March* will be played.[88]

Meanwhile, Ezra Pound has died; he had promised and even wished to read poems. Again, a meeting for which I had long hoped is shattered.

I have noted your new address,

My wife also offers her greetings.

Cordially, from my home to yours,

Yours,

Ernst Jünger

67) Martin Heidegger to Ernst Jünger, Freiburg
im Breisgau, 19 December 1972

Dear and Honored Ernst Jünger,

We thank you cordially for the small memorial book, at once vast in scope and concentrated in precious passages.

---

88. The *Heidegger March* was composed in 1969 on the occasion of Heidegger's eighty-fourth birthday by Paul Huber.

Our cordial greetings to you and your honored wife on the occasion of the celebration, with our good wishes for the coming year.

As always,

Yours,

Martin Heidegger

68) Martin Heidegger to Ernst Jünger, Freiburg im Breisgau, 15 May 1973

Dear Herr Jünger,

Cordial thanks for *The Catapult*.[89] Since I was in boarding school from 1903 to 1906 in Constance and from 1906 to 1909 here in Freiburg, I will read your book with particular interest and from presumably slightly different experiences. The students at the boarding school were then called "archepiscopal servants" and had a different structure and discipline than your "pension."

Sadly we cannot come to the celebration in Amriswil, since the complicated journey and the many public appearances are a strain in my old age. The celebration there will as always succeed most beautifully and please.

Cordially, from home to home,

Yours,

Martin Heidegger

Please send my greetings to your brother Friedrich Georg

69) Ernst Jünger to Martin Heidegger, 7941 Wiflingen, über Riedlingen, 17 November 1973

Dear, Honored Martin Heidegger,

On the occasion of your *petit rien* ["little nothing"] I, to my pleasure, have heard from you once again.[90] Many thanks! But even

---

89. Ernst Jünger, *Die Zwille* (Stuttgart: Klett, 1973).

90. Heidegger sent Jünger an offprint of a text for the inauguration of the "Messkirch Gymnasium" (that was to have been named for Heidegger) with the following dedication: "un petit rien/For/ Ernst Jünger/cordially/Martin Heidegger/ Freiburg, 5 November 1973.

greater things come—thus, today, the *Dialogue with Heidegger* by Jean Beaufret, which has just appeared in *Éditions de minuit*.[91] Paging through it allows one to anticipate that here he has accomplished a most serious work. I will offer M. Beaufret my thanks after reading it, and ask that if you should write to him, to send him advance greetings.

I should also congratulate you for having been spared patronage of this *Gymnasium*, which in normal times would have surely been named for you. Today, there is nothing more shameful than honors. After first being sent to the dogs, one ends up on a postage stamp. The entomologists number among the few whose honors still give me pleasure. An example of another *petit rien*.

Cordially, to which my wife adds her greetings, I remain

Yours,

Ernst Jünger

70) Ernst Jünger to Martin Heidegger, 7941 Wiflingen, über Riedlingen, 14 July 1974

Dear, Honored Martin Heidegger,

In *Études Polémologiques* I find an article by Hervé Savon, "Philosophy and Politics in Heidegger."[92] I do not know whether the text means something to you; in all events it will have a place in your archives. I am therefore sending you the issue now.

I have for a long time avoided bothering you with my own texts; your correspondence is extensive enough. We have missed you several times already in Amriswil, and at the soirées in Wasserschloss—only last week at a reception for Henri Michaux.[93] We therefore greeted your lovely portrait on the wall.

With cordial thanks and best wishes from home to home,

Yours,

Ernst Jünger

91. Jean Beaufret, *Dialogue avec Heidegger*, 4 volumes (Paris: Éditions de minuit, 1973–1985).

92. *Études Polémologiques. Revue français de polémologie* (Paris, 1974), n. 13: 96–99.

93. Henri Michaux (1899–1984), a Belgian author and painter.

71) Martin Heidegger to Ernst Jünger, 78
Freiburg im Breisgau/Zähringen, Fillibach 25,
15 August 1974

Dear, Honored Herr Jünger,

Many thanks for sending the journal with the article concerning "Philosophy and Politics in Heidegger." Both were up to now unknown to me. The article sadly assumed an already old erroneous translation of *Being and Time*: "Being *toward* death" as "être *pour* la mort," instead of translating it in the perspective of "*ecstatic* temporality" as "être *vers* la mort."

Your mailings are never a bother, but rather a pleasure and a profit.

At my advanced age I must be economical with my time and my powers; that is why I avoid travel and public appearances. For this reason, I probably will not receive more invitations from our Amriswil friends.

I am pleased that you are collaborating on *Crossroads*.[94] As a small gift in return, I am enclosing a picture of our "old age home," taken from our old house here.

Cordially, best wishes from home to home,

Yours,

Martin Heidegger

P. S. A special greeting to Henri Michaux

[photograph included with a handwritten note on the back; what follows is a description]:

Our old age home

In the garden next to the old house, which still accommodated my library in my former study. In my current room I have only a few texts and my unpublished manuscripts around me.

14.08.74

M. H.

72) Martin Heidegger to Ernst Jünger, after 26
September 1974

To all who participate in the effort of reflection in the present age of the world, to give thanks for your thoughts:

---

94. The journal *Scheidewege. Vierjahresschrift für skeptisches Denken* was founded in 1971 by Jünger's brother, Friedrich Georg, and Max Himmelheber.

> More founding than poetry,
> More grounding than thinking,
> Let thanks remain.
>> Those who reach gratitude
>> brings thanks back before
>>> the presence of the inaccessible,
>>> for which we—mortals all—
>>> From the in-ception
>>>> Are appropriate.

Martin Heidegger

73) Ernst Jünger to Martin Heidegger, 7941 Wiflingen, über Riedlingen, 4 October 1974

Dear, Honored Martin Heidegger,

I missed your 85th birthday while in Turkey. I belatedly join the crowd of those offering their congratulations.

You must now make for your ninetieth with your friends. *Post nubila Phoebus* already announces itself.[95] For us of course these are just questions of topography, but is still good, and perhaps it is even a general indication, when one sees things coming into order albeit externally.

With cordial wishes, for you and for your opus magnum that now begins,[96]

Yours,

Ernst Jünger

P. S. I was pleased today that Jean Beaufret sent me the third volume of his *Dialogue with Heidegger*.

---

95. See note 54.
96. In fall, 1973, work began on the preparation of Heidegger's *Gesamtausgabe*.

74) Martin Heidegger to Ernst Jünger, Freiburg, 25 March 1975

Honored, Dear Ernst Jünger,

I send cordial greetings on your eightieth birthday with the included unpublished manuscript.[97]

My particular wish for you on this day is brief:

Remain with the proven, illuminating decision on your singular path of saying.

That such saying is itself already an act that needs no supplement by a *praxis*, only few still (or yet?) understand today.

Sadly, we must abandon participating in a visit with friends, for which Herr Klett has invited us to Stuttgart, since, with my age, I must avoid every demand involving a large circle of people.

The included manuscript contains the text that I chose for a talk, which the then-President of the Berlin Academy of Art—Professor Scharoun, who has since died—had requested.[98]

Sadly, page 3 of the text has "run off" somewhere, so that I must replace the missing page with a photocopy, marked in red, from an identical redaction.

For you, and your wife, dear Herr Jünger, and also in the name of my wife, wishing a day of celebration, I think of you in all friendship.

Yours,

Martin Heidegger

75) Ernst Jünger to Martin Heidegger, 7941 Wiflingen, über Riedlingen, 8 May 1975

Dear, Honored Martin Heidegger,

It is after great delay that I thank you for your best wishes and for

---

97. Heidegger's lecture, "Die Herkunft der Kunst und die Bestimmung des Denkens" ("The Origin of Art and the Vocation of Thinking") was delivered in Athens before the Academy of Arts and Sciences, 4 April 1967. It was first published in *Distanz und Nähe. Reflexionen und Analysen zur Kunst der Gegenwart: Festschrift für Walter Biemel zum 65. Geburtstag* (*Distance and Nearness. Reflections and Analyses of Contemporary Art: Festschrift for Walter Biemel's 65 Birthday*), ed. Petra Jaeger and Rudolf Lüthe (Würzburg, 1983), 11–22. It was later included in *Denkerfahrungen. 1910–1976*, ed. Hermann Heidegger (Frankfurt am Main: Klostermann, 1983). It appears in Heidegger's *Gesamtausgabe*, vol. 80.

98. The architect Hans Scharoun (1893–1972), President of the Academy of Fine Art in Berlin from 1955 to 1958.

the exquisite gift—but you know from your own experience how things go at home on such a day.

Your manuscript has already given me great satisfaction, if only for its graphic style; it will be in good hands with me.

Herr Himmelheber, who together with my brother Friedrich Georg edits the *Crossroads*, already asked if it is free to be published there.[99] That is a question only the author can answer.

The spring has begun late this year. With the rising of the sun I wish you continued good health and creative power. It would be lovely to see you once again in the course of the year. Our common friends report to me from time to time about how you are faring.

With cordial greetings, also to your wife

Yours,

Ernst Jünger

76) Elfride Heidegger to Ernst Jünger, 16 June 1976[100]

Dear Herr Jünger,

In the Hölderlin volume that my husband constantly had lying next to him in his final weeks, I found a slip of paper that I allowed to be photocopied—only ten times—for family and close friends. Please accept this sheet in memory of M. H.

Thank you and your wife for your presence at the grave.

Yours,

Elfride Heidegger

[Martin Heidegger's paper, included by Elfride Heidegger]:

Hölderlin's Words

Taken from Volume IV of his works,
That Norbert von Hellingrath compiled—
To be spoken slowly and simply

---

99. Max Himmelheber (1904–2000), a German industrialist and inventor of particle board.

100. Heidegger died at his home on 26 May 1976; he was buried in Messkirch on 28 May.

as final greeting from my grave:
for Elfride, the children and grandchildren, for
my brother Fritz and his sons,
for Clothilde and her children,
and my closest friends[101]
1 *Bread and Wine* Strophe 4 v. 55–62, p. 121
2 *To the Germans* Strophes 1 and 2, p. 132
3 *Conciliator* . . . v. 1–13, p. 162
4 *The Titans* v. 1–3, p. 208
5 *Bread and Wine* Strophe 3 v. 41–46, p. 120/21

Bread and Wine
4 Strophe, v. 55–62

O happy Greece! You home to all the celestials,
Is it then true what we first heard in our youth?
Festive hall! Your floor is sea, and mountains your tables,
Truly built long ago but for a single use.
But where the thrones, the temple, and where the jugs
Brimming with nectar, the songs to charm the gods?
Where, now, the shining oracles wandering far?
Delphi sleeps; where does great destiny sound?

To the Germans
1 and 2 Strophe

Never mock the child, who pricks and spurs
The wooden horse and thinks himself so brave,
O, good friends! Even we are
Poor in deeds and fertile in our minds.

But comes the deed, as the beam comes from the sky,
From thought, perhaps, intelligent and ripe?
Follows the fruit, as from the groves
The somber foliage, the silent script?

---

101. These fragments of Hölderlin's poems were read at graveside by Hermann Heidegger. Clothilde Rapp née Oschwald (b. 1923), is Heidegger's niece, the daughter of his sister, Maria Oschwald née Heidegger (1892–1956).

The Conciliator, Who Never Believed . . .
v. 1–13

Conciliator, who never believed
Are here now, a friendly form to me,
Immortal, but indeed
I recognize the high one
That bends my knees,
And almost like a blind man I must,
Messenger from heaven, ask you why
And whence you've come to me, happy peace!
This much I know, mortal you are not,
For much may a wise man or
A faithful one, true-sighted friends, reveal,
But when a god appears, from heaven and earth and sea,
Comes then a clarity, ever-new.

The Titans
v. 1–3

It is not yet
Time. Still they are
Unbound. The indifferent care nothing for the divine.

Bread and Wine
3 Strophe, v. 41–46

So come! That we may look at open spaces,
That we seek what is our own, 'though it be far.
One thing stands fast; it is at noon, or nearly
Midnight, always there is a measure,
Common to all, yet to each his own is given,
All must come and go wherever he can.

CORRESPONDENCE BETWEEN ERNST JÜNGER AND HERMANN HEIDEGGER

1) Hermann Heidegger to Ernst Jünger, 15 December 1981

Dear, Honored Herr Jünger,

As you presumably know, my father entrusted me with the management of his estate and with the care of his collected works.

From your letter to my father of 8.5.1975 I infer that he had presented you a manuscript for your 80th birthday. The question posed in your letter, whether the manuscript is free for publication—Herr Himmelheber asked this—my father probably never answered.

I would be grateful to receive a photocopy of this manuscript, of which I was unaware, in order to be able to judge where in the collected works it should appear.

May I take this opportunity to ask how many of my father's letters and postcards are in your possession, and whether it is possible that you received one additional manuscript early in the year from my father?

12 letters and postcards of yours from the years 1964–1974 are located in the Heidegger Archive in Marbach. A few more letters were inserted by my father in your books, which are still in the library at Rötebuck.

My father determined that his letters should be published first in section IV within the framework of the *Gesamtausgabe*. Hitherto, 14 volumes of the *Gesamtausgabe* have appeared. There are still a few years before sections I and II are finished.

My rapidly aging and nearly blind mother, who nevertheless still participates intellectually in everything, sends you her cordial greetings.

With good wishes for you
And with most cordial greetings
I am most humbly yours
Hermann Heidegger

2) Herman Heidegger to Ernst Jünger Stegen, 26 March 1985

Most honored Herr Jünger,

For your 90th birthday I am sending you, in the name of my mother who can no longer write, but is still completely present intellectually, an abundance of good wishes: May you preserve your intellectual and physical energy for years hence, so that we will still be able to profit for a long time from the results of your work—a work that perhaps will be rightly honored in Germany only in the next century.

I have learned with pleasure, during four weeks in Marbach, that copies of your letters with my father were exchanged between Marbach and you. I do not yet know the title and content of the manuscript that my father had sent you for your 80th birthday. Would you be so kind as to allow the opportunity to send a copy of this manuscript to Marbach?

In the hope that you are in good health, and that together with your honored wife and with many good, old friends, you are able to enjoy an all-round lovely birthday, I remain

Respectfully,
Your very devoted
Hermann Heidegger

3) Ernst Jünger to Hermann Heidegger

"Fundamentally, we are all collective beings, for how little we possess and how little we are that in the purest sense we call our property. We must all receive and learn from those who were before us, as well as from those who are with us."

Goethe

I thank all those from whom I have been able to learn, and today in particular, thank all who thought of me so kindly on my 90th birthday, for their good wishes and their lovely gifts. They have brought me much joy.

[handwritten inclusion of Jünger's]:

I will have the manuscript photocopied soon for Marbach.

Wilflingen, 29 March 1985
Ernst Jünger

Part Two

ERNST JÜNGER'S ESSAY, ACROSS THE LINE

Across the Line

1

In the Preface to *Will to Power*, Nietzsche describes himself as "Europe's first absolute nihilist who, however, has already lived through nihilism within himself—leaving it behind, beneath, outside himself."[1]

He then notes that his work announces a cautionary movement, which "in some future or other" will abolish this absolute nihilism, even while presupposing that it is necessary.

Although more than sixty years have passed since these thoughts were conceived, they still excite us as statements that concern our destiny. Meanwhile, they have been filled with content, with life lived, with deeds and sufferings. The spiritual adventure was confirmed and reprised in reality.

When we look back at that statement from our present standpoint it seems to express an optimism that later observers lack. Nihilism is not considered an end, but rather as a phase in a comprehensive spiritual process, a phase which culture in its historical course, but also the individual in his personal existence, can leave behind and be done with, or perhaps even overgrow, like a scab.

Later observers, as I mentioned, will not share this favorable prognosis. Proximity to the massif only renders its details clearer, not its scale. Furthermore, within the full development of active nihilism, what is in the foreground of the decline is too stark to allow room for considera-

---

1. See *Will to Power*, Preface, §3, *Kritische Studien Ausgabe* (Berlin: De Gruyter, 1990), 13: 11 [411], 190.

tions that transcend the nightmare world. Fire, terror, suffering dominate, if only for a while. Admittedly, the spirit is unable to carry out *the* insight in the thrall of catastrophe; and there is barely any comfort in this insight. What good could it do to tell the Trojans, at the moment when the palaces of Ilium fell, that Aeneas would found a new empire? On either side of catastrophes, we may direct our view to the future and investigate the ways that lead there—yet in their maelstrom the present reigns.

2

Twenty years earlier, Dostoevsky finished his story *Raskolnikov*, which appeared in the *Russian Messenger* in 1886.[2] For a long time, this creation has rightly been seen as another major source for understanding nihilism. The object of consideration is exactly the same as in *The Will to Power*; the difference, on the other hand, is the perspective of the observer. The German's eye is directed to the spiritual and constructive standard of measurement, and a feeling of daring, of higher adventures accompanies his view. The Russian, on the other hand, considers the moral and theological content. Nietzsche mentions Dostoevsky briefly and can only have been acquainted with a portion of his work, above all with its psychology, that is, he was fascinated by the masterly technique.

Both authors have been compared several times to Napoleon. A particular work of Walter Schubart does this most thoroughly.[3] The comparison is obvious, since in *The Will to Power* as well as in *Raskolnikov* the reference to Napoleon plays a meaningful role. The great individual freed from the last shackles of the eighteenth century is seen on the one hand in the light, on the other in the shadows—here relishing a new,

---

2. Jünger consistently refers to Dostoevsky's *Crime and Punishment* as "Raskolnikov." The *Russian Messenger* was a journal published intermittently throughout the nineteenth and twentieth centuries. In addition to *Crime and Punishment*, it also published Dostoevsky's *The Idiot*, *The Possessed*, and *The Brothers Karamazov*.

3. Walter Schubart (1897–1941), *Dostojevski und Nietzsche: Symbolik ihres Lebens* (Luzern: Vita Nova, 1939). In this work, Schubart understood the religious dimensions of Dostoevski's works as a counterbalance to Nietzsche's atheism.

turbulent power, and there in a suffering inseparable from this power. Both processes are complementary, like photographic positive and negative exposures representing spiritual reality.

It ought to be seen as a favorable sign that both authors agree in their prognoses. With Dostoevsky, the prognosis is also optimistic; he does not see in nihilism a final, deadly stage. He regards it rather as curable, and indeed as curable through suffering. The fate of Raskolnikov offers in miniature a preview of the great transformation in which millions participated. Here too one has the impression that nihilism is conceived as a necessary stage, intrinsic to a movement directed toward particular ends.

3

The question that intrudes immediately upon every judgment of the situation, in every conversation and every private musing about the future, concerns what point the movement has since reached. Admittedly, the answer will continually be open to argument, however it might be formulated and supported. The reason is that it depends less on the facts of the matter than on the overall attunement toward and perspective on life. This makes the question revealing again, in a different and more compelling way.

The optimism, or even the pessimism, of such a response is entwined in proofs, but is not based upon them. It is a matter of differences of degree; for optimism, the power of persuasion rests in profundity, for proof, in clarity. Optimism can reach levels where the future is slumbering and fecund. In this case one encounters it as a knowledge that reaches more deeply than the authority of facts—and that can even create facts. Its center of gravity lies in character rather than in the world. This sort of optimism is intrinsically valuable, in so far as its supporters are animated by the will, the hope, and even the promise of enduring the eddies of history and its dangers. This is not negligible.

4

Pessimism should not be looked at as the contrary to this optimism. Catastrophe is surrounded by pessimistic currents, in particular, cur-

rents of cultural pessimism. Pessimism can be expressed, as with Burckhardt, as disgust in the face of what one sees coming—then one shifts
one's eyes toward more beautiful, although past, images.[4] Then there
are shifts to optimism, as with Bernanos—the light flares up when the
darkness is complete.[5] The absolute superiority of the enemy is precisely what speaks against it. Finally, there is a pessimism that,
although knowing that the bar has been lowered, considers greatness to
be possible even on the new level, and especially prizes the tenacity of
those who remain at their post even though all is lost. Therein lie
Spengler's merits.

The contrary to optimism, extraordinarily common today, is much
rather defeatism. One no longer has anything to set against what he
sees coming, neither in the way of values nor in the way of inner power.
In this mood, panic finds nothing to resist it; it spreads like a whirlwind.
The cruelty of the enemy, the fearsomeness of his methods, appears to
increase in the same measure in which weakness grows in man. At last,
terror surrounds him like an element. In this condition, the rumor of
nihilism already wears him down, preparing him for his ruin. Greedily,
fear seizes him, increasing terror without measure, ever on the hunt for
him.

"Have you heard of Holofernes' latest atrocity?" one citizen asks
another by way of greeting in Hebbel's *Judith*.[6] The piece generally fits
well with the mood of nihilistic rumor that accompanies terrifying figures like Nebuchadnezzar and his methods. Holofernes is said to think
himself merciful when the embers of a single city are enough for him
to polish his sword and roast his dinner. "It's fortunate that the walls
and towers have no eyes! They would collapse before such horrors, if
they could see them."

This then provokes the hubris of those with power. For all powers
who wish to spread fear, the nihilistic insinuation is the most forceful
means of propaganda. It works no less for inspiring terror within as it

---

4. Jacob Burckhardt (1818–1897), a German art historian whose work especially
influenced Nietzsche's understanding of the superiority of Greek antiquity to
modernity.

5. Georges Bernanos (1888–1948), a French Catholic author opposed to liberalism and the rise of the bourgeoisie in France, which he believed had led to France's
moral and political decline.

6. Christian Friedrich Hebbel (1813–1863), a German poet and dramatist.

does for terror directed externally. The former is above all anxious to proclaim the superior strength that society possesses over the individual. It must first of all bring itself to consciousness morally: "The people is all; you are nothing," and at the same time it must always be present to the mind as a physical threat, as total spatial and temporal proximity of deprivation and liquidation. In this situation fear performs even better than force; rumors are more valuable than facts. The indeterminate is more menacing. For this reason the apparatus of fear is readily hidden, and its sites are moved into the wilderness.

States mutually threaten one another with the other, external terror; to them it depends on a gorgon-like effect, on that unholy aura that weapons emanate when displayed from a distance—even if they are only suspected. Here too they bank on a fear that must grow to visions of apocalypse. They must make the enemy believe that they are capable of bringing about the collapse of worlds. An initial example is the propaganda that preceded the launching of flying bombs against England, which resembled the dark harbinger of cosmic disaster.

Meanwhile, the methods have been strengthened, both in scope and in refinement. They must show that one possesses unlimited power, and that one is not afraid to unleash it in conflict. In this contest one strives for a pairing of physical and ideological superiority that must radiate to the furthest borders, even if no actions are underway. They are scarcely even desirable—in such situations wars can resemble enormous traffic accidents that everyone tries to avoid. Cases are therefore possible, in which one of the partners is no longer able to sustain the tension and breaks apart without recourse to external force. Those stages in particular that are called a war of nerves aim at this effect. This sort of breakdown, as Sartre has described in *Le Sursis*, always presupposes a sum of individual breakdowns.[7] The state becomes hollow not only in its leaders, but above all in its anonymous layers. The individual is embraced by and succumbs to the spell of nihilistic tension. It is therefore valuable to investigate what behavior can be recommended to him in this challenge. His interiority is after all the genuine forum of this

---

7. *Le Sursis* (*The Reprieve*) is a novel by Jean-Paul Sartre published in 1945 concerning the eight days prior to the Munich Agreement and the consequent takeover of Czekoslovakia in 1938. It is the second installment of his trilogy *Les chemins de la liberté* (*The Roads to Freedom*).

world; and his decision is more important than that of dictators and those with power. It is their presupposition.

5

In the meantime, before we turn to this problem, there are some preparatory diagnostic remarks to make. The concept of nihilism is, at present, not only one of the least settled and most controversial. It is also used in a polemical sense. One must however sense nihilism as a grand destiny, a fundamental power whose influence no one can avoid.

Close together with the invasive character of nihilism is the fact that it is impossible to be touched by the Absolute, if one disregards sacrifice. Here there are no saints. Neither are there perfect works of art. Likewise, one finds no supreme thought by which things are ordered, although there is no lack of plans; the princely form of men is lacking. Even in morals one recognizes a provisional character, which in *The Worker* we called the character of the factory. Morally, we are instructed either by the past or by something still uncertain, something that is coming to be. Therein lies the conflict, and in particular the confusing language of rights.

A good definition of nihilism would be comparable to discovering the causes of cancer. It would not mean a cure, but rather its requirements, as far as individuals in general cooperate in them. Indeed, it is about a process that spreads far beyond history.

If we consult both masters introduced at the outset, we find in Nietzsche the view that nihilism is the expression of the devaluation of the highest values. In this state, he calls nihilism normal, but as a transitional state, pathological—a good distinction, implying that one can behave sensibly in what concerns one's current state. This is not the case concerning the past and the future; here, the meaningless and the hopeless obtrude. The decline of values is above all the decline of Christian values; it corresponds to the impossibility of bringing forth higher types, or even conceiving of them, and flows into pessimism. This pessimism develops into nihilism when hierarchy, at first disillusioning, comes to be treated with hatred and rejected. There remain only the values of judgment, and therefore of critique: the weak are broken by them, while the stronger destroy what does not break, and the strongest overcome the values of judgment and exceed them. Nihilism can be as much a sign of the weakness as of the strength. It is the expression of the uselessness of the other world, not however of the world and of existence in general. Great growth brings with it immense damage and loss, and in this respect, nihilism's appearing as the most extreme form of pessimism can be a favorable sign.

For Dostoevsky, nihilism becomes effective in the isolation of the individual, in his exit from community, which is essentially a religious communion. Active nihilism prepares itself like an eruption, as in the weeks Raskolnikov spends alone in his coffin-like chamber. It leads to an increase in physical and spiritual power at the expense of well-being. It can culminate in a horrific death, as is described in the fate of the student Hippolyte in *The Idiot*. It may even conclude with suicide, as with Smerdyakov in the *Karamazovs*, with Stavrogin in the *Devils*, or with Svidrigailov in *Crime and Punishment*, as one also fears in the case of Ivan Karamazov and with many others. In the best case it will lead to healing, when after a public confession of guilt one reenters the community. Through purification in the inferno or in *The House of the Dead*, one can attain a higher level than before entering into nihilism.

The inherent affinities between both conceptions are undeniable. They advance in the same three phases: from doubt to pessimism, from there to actions in valueless and godless space, and then to new fulfillment. This allows us to conclude that we are seeing one and the same reality, although from quite distant points.

6

The difficulty in defining nihilism lies in the fact that it is impossible for the spirit to gain a representation of Nothing. It approaches the zone in which intuition as well as knowledge wither: the two great means by which it is directed. One makes of Nothing neither image nor concept.

Thus is nihilism placed in relation only to the outer belt of nothing, to the margins of Nothing, but never to the basic power itself. In a similar way one can experience dying, but not death. While immediate contact with Nothing is indeed conceivable, swift annihilation must follow, as if a spark jumped from the Absolute. Malraux and Bernanos occasionally describe it, mostly in connection with sudden suicide.

There is a moment of certainty that existence has become impossible—then the heartbeat, the circulation, the secretion of the kidneys, proceed as meaninglessly as the ticking of a clock to a corpse. Then a gruesome putrefaction would be the consequence. Stavrogin foresees this concerning his stay in Switzerland and chooses the rope. He already anticipates the dangers bound up with safeguarding basic security.

The particulars of annihilation are not only described in literature but also exhibited. The artist does not just choose destruction as his theme; he identifies with it himself. It penetrates his language, his colors. That is the difference between a literature of pure revulsion and naturalism, in which optimism still rules in spite of all the ugly objects.

7

To get an image of nihilism, one does well first of all to eliminate phenomena that appear in its culture or its wake, and which are therefore readily mixed up with it. They are above all what give the word a polemical sense. Among them number the three great domains, of illness, of evil, and of chaos.

Beginning with the third, it is not difficult for us today, as a result of hard-won experience, to grasp the difference between the nihilistic and the chaotic. It is however important, since one has to decide between chaos and Nothing.

It has been shown that nihilism can harmonize with vast systems of order, which is even the rule when it is active and its power deployed. Order is a favorable substrate for nihilism; nihilism refashions order for its purposes. Provided merely that order is abstract and thus intellectual—here in the first place belongs the developed state with its officials and apparatchiks, and above all at a time when sustaining ideas with their nomos and ethos have been lost or are in decay, although they are perhaps still alive in the foreground, more visible than ever. Then, one only considers what ought to be actualized, a condition to which there corresponds a species of journalistic historical writing.

Strictly linked with this development, in which the state becomes the nihilistic object, is the appearance of mass urban parties, as rational as they are passionate. In the case of their followers, they can become so similar to the state that it is difficult to distinguish between them. The victorious power in a civil war constructs organs that correspond to those of the state, which infiltrate it, or leech off it. Finally there arise deformities.

Something quite similar can be observed in armies, that they become all the more fit for nihilistic action the more the old nomos, which it conceives as tradition, fades. In the same way, the pure character of order and instrumentality must grow, and as a result the possibility for anyone whose hand is on the lever to use the army arbitrarily.

Because armies always preserve in themselves ancient elements, the evolution will be less rending where the army serves as a means for change. Even when they intervene in politics, represented by generals, their chances for success are less than when mass parties drive things. The propensity to encumber the movement with old personages and values endangers the pace of nihilistic action. One could posit the maxim that in such a situation a general must either be entirely superior like Caesar, or totally insignificant.

Above all, technical order is suitable for any promotion and subordination, although precisely by this subordination it alters the powers that serve it by making them into workers. Technical order simulates the necessary measure of emptiness to which any content can be given. This is equally true of the organizations that attach themselves to it—federations, groups, health insurance plans, trade unions and others. They are all arranged for pure functioning, whose ideal seems to be that one need only to "press the button" or "flip the switch." They therefore adapt themselves without any transition to apparently opposing powers. Quite early on, Marxism saw a favorable medium in developing capitalist trusts and monopolies. With increasing automatism armies gain an insect-like perfection. They fight on in situations that older styles of warfare would consider criminal. Then the conqueror recruits troops from them under a new banner. Indeed, loyalty will not be very meaningful, when compulsion is refined to a science.

Similarly, one sees that individuals fall more easily under the sway of any powers, the more they absorb the elements of order. One is familiar with the reproaches that are raised against officials, judges, generals, and teachers. They are directed against a drama that returns as soon as it comes to a revolution. Indeed, one cannot turn the elements of society into pure functions and expect that their ethos will remain.

The virtue of the functionary is that he functions, and it is good when in quieter times one harbors no illusions about this point.

This may be enough to indicate that nihilism can in fact harmonize with vast worlds of order, and that it even needs them in order to become active on a large scale. Chaos is first observable when nihilism comes to fail in one of its constellations. Even within catastrophes it is informative how far, indeed how even almost to the last, the elements of order remain. That shows perhaps that order is not only compatible with nihilism, but composes its style.

Chaos, therefore, is at most a consequence of nihilism, and not even the worst one. It remains crucial to understand how much genuine anarchy is hidden in chaos, and with it, how much wild fecundity. It is to be sought in individuals and in society, but not in the wreckage into which the state fragments. The aphorisms in *Zarathustra* directed against the "draconian State," and in particular the idea of the eternal return, are clearly suggestions that for Nietzsche nihilism has not penetrated into the depths.[8] The anarchist will often have a relation to the perfect and the good, and in his best instance he resembles more the first than the "last man"; the nihilist will even regard him immediately as an opponent as soon as he comes to dominate.[9] In the Spanish Civil War there was even an anarchist group that was equally persecuted by the Reds and the Whites.[10]

Let us conceive of the difference between chaos and anarchy as the difference between the disorder of the uninhabited and the disorder of the living. Desert and primeval forest would be models. In this sense chaos is not necessary for the nihilist; it is not a place on which he depends. Still less does anarchy suit him. It would disrupt the strict sequence by which he moves. The same is true of intoxication. Even in places where nihilism shows its most uncanny features, as in the great sites of physical annihilation, sobriety, hygiene and strict order rule to the end.

---

8. See *Thus Spoke Zarathustra* Book I.1: "The Three Metamorphoses."

9. See *Thus Spoke Zarathustra*, Prologue, §5.

10. During the Spanish Civil War (1936–1939) the Republican or Loyalist faction was known as "the Reds," while Franco's Nationalist party was known as "the Whites."

8

Similarly, one must address the opinion that nihilism is a disease with caution. With a bit of observation, one will find that physical health is connected with it—above all, where it is vigorously at work. With passive nihilism it is different. The dialectical play of increasing sensitivity and increasingly powerful actions that move our age is based upon it. Primarily, one cannot maintain that nihilism is based upon disease, nor even upon decadence, although both are certainly found there in abundance.

If one considers the immense efforts of work and of will that the active nihilist demands of himself, his disdain for pity and pain, the fluctuations from high to low temperatures to which he exposes himself, and the cult of the body and its worldly powers that one ordinarily finds in him, one must admit that he has received the gift of good health. And in fact one can discover that he has established a level of performance that he demands of himself and others absolutely. In this, he is not unlike the Jacobin who can be considered one of his precursors.

Nevertheless, it is peculiar that such Cyclopes and Titans emerge in a world in which caution is increasing in the extreme, and where one wants to avoid even the slightest draft. Meanwhile, in the welfare state, with its entitlements, health insurance, safety nets and narcotics, one sees types emerging, whose skin is tanned like leather and whose skeleton seems to be of iron. It may be that these are complementary figures, in the sense of color theory; the general weakening of nerve requires it. One inquires about their schools, about what has shaped them. They are surely diverse.

In the first place, one can recognize the school of civil war—the life of the political nihilists and social revolutionaries, the camps and prisons, Siberia. With them also belong, like a mirror image, the dispossessed, the degraded, the disgraced, escapees from the waves of terror, purges and liquidations. One sees here the one and there the other triumphant, or even, as in Spain, at a stalemate. What is common in all these encounters is their complete mercilessness. The adversary is no longer seen as a man; he stands outside the law.

The material battles of the First World War form the other source. It brought forth a man of iron and with him a new style of action and a series of frontist movements, which the failed policy confronted helplessly. One can foresee that the Second World War, in particular in Germany and Russia, will produce persons similarly formed. In the experience, the knowledge of those years spent in the East, including the fate of prisoners, there lies a still uninvestigated chapter of pain, the authentic currency of our age.

Finally, important in this connection is that special type of work called sport. It manifests the aspiration not just to normalize a higher degree of physical health, but to enter the record books at the limits of the possible, even to exceed them. In alpine skiing, flying, ski jumping, there are demands that surpass the human and an automatism preceded by deadening. Such records raise the bar over and over again. This process even translates to the workplace; it produces those worker-heroes who master twenty times over the work quota of a single exploited worker of 1913.

Considered from this point of view, one cannot blame illness, decadence or *morbidezza* for this development. Instead, one sees men appear who go their way like iron machines, indifferent even when the catastrophe breaks them. Admittedly, the spectacle remains rather strange, in which currents of activity and passivity touch, while the plankton sinks to the bottom and sharks rise up—on the one hand, the most tender impressionism, on the other, explosive action; on the one hand, subtle and pained understanding, on the other, will and excessive development of power.

All this also plays out in literature, even earlier, and in fact with more uniformity and clarity than its contemporaries suspect. The great theme of the last hundred years is nihilism, regardless of whether it enters discourse in its active or passive forms. In this respect it is irrelevant to the value of the work whether it is by weakness or power: they are variations in one and the same play. In authors as different as Verlaine, Proust, Trakl, Rilke, and even in Lautréamont, Nietzsche, Rimbaud, and Barrès, much is nevertheless the same. The work of Joseph Conrad is noteworthy for the way resignation and action are kept in balance and rigorously intertwined. But pain is present in one as in another, and probably courage as well. The great turning point lies in the fact that annihilation is first felt in suffering. Often this brings an ultimate beauty, like the first frost in forests, and a refinement that is unavailable to classical ages. Then the theme shifts into resistance; it poses the question of how a person faced with annihilation, can endure in the wake of nihilism. That is the change that includes us; it is the concern of our literature. One could cite countless names—for example, to name a few, Wolfe, Faulkner, Malraux, T. E. Lawrence, René Quinton, Bernanos, Hemingway, Saint-Exupéry, Kafka, Spengler, Benn, Montherlant and Graham Greene. The experimental is common to all of them, a provisional attitude and awareness of the dangerous situation, the great menace, two traits that determine style over and above languages, peoples, and empires—for there can be no doubt about the fact that such a style exists and is not alive only in technology.

One could add that to a comprehensive account of an age belongs the knowledge of its extreme wings, in the present case therefore knowledge of the passive as well as the active encounter with Nothing. This double hold explains the effect that Nietzsche has upon our minds.

9

So much for individuals and their health. Should it be any different with peoples and races? One should probably answer no, since one could hardly assert that nihilism is unique to old peoples. A kind of skepticism lives in them that protects them. On fresh, young trunks nihilism, once grafted, will assert itself more strongly. It takes over the primitive, the indifferent, and the uncultivated more powerfully than it does a world gifted with history, tradition and critical powers. Such domains will also be more difficult to automate. On the contrary, primitive forces send out shoots into the graft. Thus, one is thrust into a kind of fever, which grips not only mechanical technology, but also nihilistic theory. It becomes an ersatz religion. Nineteenth-century professorial theories become sacrosanct. For reasons of security it is recommended that today's tourist understand the point to which the Enlightenment has advanced in the individual countries he visits, or where it has paused.

If one ever has the opportunity to consider a nihilistic guild from up close—one does not need to think of a group of bomb-throwers or a death's-head regiment, but perhaps a collection of doctors, technicians or economists, occupied with appropriate questions—then he will indeed be able to make several observations, although hardly of a particular illness.

It is also certain that illness increases. The immense number of doctors already indicates this. There is a nihilistic medicine, whose characteristics lie in the fact that it does not want to heal, but pursues other ends, and this school spreads. It corresponds to a patient who wishes to persist in his illness. On the other hand one can speak of a special health belonging to the sphere of nihilistic phenomena, of a fresh propaganda, which gives a vivid impression of physical harmlessness. One encounters it as much in the privileged strata as in the phases of the economic cycle that are tied to comfort.

Nietzsche was correct, that nihilism is a normal condition, and pathological only when one compares it with values that are no longer or not yet in effect. As a normal condition it compasses health and illness in a peculiar manner. In another passage, Nietzsche uses the image of a lukewarm winter wind, as a result of which, where once one could travel, soon no one will be able to go any longer. The image is good; nihilism, in its destructive and future-laden violence, recalls a warm wind coming down from the mountains. The effect on systems is quite similar—one paralyzed, another livelier in its wellbeing and spirituality. One knows that in many lands offenses are judged more mildly, if they are committed when the warm Alpine wind blows.

10

This leads us to the third distinction, namely, the one that must be drawn between nihilism and evil. Evil does not need to appear in it—especially where security is established. When catastrophe threatens, evil will be the brother of Chaos. It then appears as a secondary phenomenon, like a fire in a theater or the sinking of a ship.

On the other hand, plans and programs for nihilistic action can be distinguished by good intentions and philanthropy. Often they already follow as a counterblow to the initial disorders, with the inclination to save, and nevertheless they only prolong them by aggravating the processes that have taken shape. This then leads to the fact that the extremes of right and wrong become almost indistinguishable more so to men of action than to those who are passive.

Even with great crimes evil barely appears as a motive; there would have to be a villain who takes advantage of the nihilistic process. Natures of this sort are rather disruptive agents. Indifference is more suitable. Men with past criminal histories who become dangerous are less disturbing than those types one sees on every street corner and behind every counter, who have entered into a sort of moral automation. This points to a drop in the climate. When the weather improves, one sees the same beings peacefully returning to the usual places. The nihilist is no criminal in the traditional sense, since there would then still have to be a valid order. For the same reasons, however, crime is irrelevant to him; he passes over from moral connection to automatic ones. Where nihilism becomes the normal condition, the only choice that still remains for the individual is between kinds of injustice. Nevertheless, value judgments cannot come from places where one is not yet part of the process. The new flood will more likely arise from the depths.

If one could address nihilism as a specific evil, the diagnosis would be more favorable. There are proven remedies against evil. More disturbing is the fusion, indeed the total confusion of good and evil, which often eludes the sharpest eye.

11

We will not touch upon the highest hope that is contained in this age. If the words of Hölderlin are true, then salvation must grow in force. Meaninglessness pales at its first rays.

We are now more captivated by the effects of the change that is moving forward, unnoticed by the masses. Here perhaps one finds useful indications amid currents of nihilism. It is therefore necessary to portray the symptoms and not the causes.

In these symptoms one is struck at first glance by an essential characteristic, which one could call reduction. The nihilistic world is in its essence a reduced and increasingly self-reductive world, which necessarily corresponds to the movement to the null point. The most basic sentiment that reigns in it is that of reduction and of becoming reduced. Against it, romanticism no longer prevails, but only echoes a vanished reality. Profusion dries up; the individual feels himself exploited in multifarious, not merely economic, ways.

The reduction can be spatial, intellectual, spiritual; it can touch the beautiful, the good, the true, economics, health, politics—only in the end it will always be perceived as a loss. That does not exclude the fact that it is tied for long stretches to the growing development and dispersion of power. We see this above all in the simplification of scientific theory. It eliminates perspectives at the expense of dimensions. That procedure leads to chains of conclusions, as one can study rather well in Darwinism. Characteristic of nihilistic thinking is also the inclination to reduce the world with its complicated and multifaceted tendencies to a common denominator. It seems impressive, if only for a little while. It is taught, since its dialectic is the best means to demolish the opponent who is without reserves. Then, however, the one attacked also adopts the methodology. This is the basis for the intellectual pace of reaction. The means may in certain phases of nihilistic development become unavoidable; at bottom it remains a sign of reduction.

12

To these signs one can further add the disappearance of the wonderful, and with it not only the forms of admiration, but also amazement as source for science disappear. What in this context one calls admiration or amazement is above all the impression of a figure in the world of space and number. Then the immense strikes one everywhere—it corresponds to the exact science, which is finally reduced to the mere art of measurement. Dizziness before the cosmic abyss is an aspect of nihilism. It can awaken sublimity as in "Eureka," by E. A. Poe, even though a particular and specific fear of Nothing will always be connected with it.[11]

Léon Bloy has already placed the acceleration of movement in strict correspondence with this kind of fear.[12] He traces back the invention of

---

11. *Eureka*, subtitled "An Essay on the Material and Spiritual Universe," was a prose poem composed by Edgar Allen Poe in 1848. He dedicated it to Alexander von Humbolt (1769–1859).

12. Léon Bloy (1846–1917) was a French novelist, essayist, and poet. His first novel, *Le Désespéré* (1887), was an assault on modern rationalism.

ever faster machines to the will to flight, to a kind of instinct that alerts the individual to menaces in the face of which he must perhaps hastily flee from one part of the earth to another. This then would be the counterpart, the dark side of the will to power: the perception of emptiness that precedes the typhoon. With every acceleration of movement a reduction takes place. Similar to rich natural deposits and veins, repose is excavated and completely transformed into movement.

A related sign one must grasp is the growing tendency toward specialization, toward separateness and passing over into isolation. This even occurs in the humanities, where the synoptic talent dwindles almost completely, just as higher handicraft disappears from the world of work. Specialization goes so far that the individual only expands upon a derivative idea, only makes a handle in the assembly line. There is no lack of theories that seek in specialization the cause of the withering manifest in personalities; yet the opposite is true, and for this reason the remedies prescribed for it do not go deeply enough.

This isolation, unsettling to the sciences and to praxis, but which also accelerates their revolution, corresponds in morality to the relation to the lower values. The fact that the "highest values devalue themselves" leads to new incursions into the now vacant region. Such attempts may be carried out in the Church as well as in every other area. A reductive incursion betrays itself, for example, when God is conceived as "the good" or where ideas float in a void.

Countless ersatz religions arise, as under a heaven of lesser gods. One can even say that through the dethroning of the highest values, it now becomes possible each and every thing to be illuminated and given meaning in a cult. Not only do the natural sciences enter into this role. Worldviews and sects prosper; it is an age of apostles without mandates. Finally, the political parties participate in the apotheosis, and whatever serves their doctrines and their changing goals becomes divine.

13

We could cite even more fields where the withering is manifest, perhaps in art or eroticism. It has to do with a process that attacks the whole, and finally leads to the most diminished, graying or exhausted landscapes. In the best case crystallization arises. What is peculiar to this is not its novelty. It is rather the way it embraces the entire world. For the first time we observe nihilism becoming a style.

Often enough, in human history, in individuals and in groups both small and large, the collapse of immortal hierarchies and its consequences become visible. There have always then existed powerful reserves at one's disposal, whether in the elementary world or the educated world. Untamed ground existed in its fullness, and entire cultures remained undisturbed. Today a withering seizes the entire world, which indeed is not merely a withering, but is at the same time an acceleration, simplification, intensification, and rush toward unknown goals.

When one examines the negative side of reduction, perhaps the most significant of its characteristics is the reduction of the number to the figure, or of symbols to the barest relations. It generates the impression of a desert filled with prayer wheels, circling under the starry heavens. Incessantly, the measurability of all relations become most important. One still consecrates, although one no longer believes in transubstantiation. Then one reinterprets it, making it more understandable.

An early type is the dandy; he still has at his disposal the external dimensions of a culture whose meaning begins to wither away. Prostitution accompanies this, as sexuality denuded of symbols. It then becomes not only marketable, but also measurable. The beautiful, estimable in figures, becomes common to all. The most comprehensive reduction is to pure causality; among its subordinate types counts the economic treatment of the historical and social world. Little by little all areas can be brought down to this common denominator, even places as foreign to causality as the dream.

Here we touch upon the dismantling of taboos, which at first frightens, alienates and perhaps even excites. What has then been enucleated becomes a matter of course. At first, motorizing hearses is daring; then it becomes an economic fact. Today as macabre a book as Evelyn Waugh writes about the Hollywood funeral industry belongs to entertainment literature.[13] The daring lies always only at the beginnings. In the meantime a sort of culmination is produced that robs participation in the great process of nihilism of its charm.

On what is the discord based that threatens to erode the ground

---

13. Evelyn Waugh, *The Loved One* (Boston and Toronto: Little, Brown, and Company, 1948).

beneath the radical parties, and which distinguishes so meaningfully the years after 1945 from those after 1918? The reason is to be supposed in the fact that we have passed the zero point, not only ideologically, but also at the core of the ideology. This then brings a new direction of the spirit and the perception of new phenomena.

14

One can scarcely expect these phenomena to appear in a surprising or dazzling way. Crossing over the line, the passage of the zero point *divides* the drama; it indicates the midpoint, but not the end. Security is still quite far away. Hope for it will be possible. The barometer reading improves in spite of external dangers, and that is better than having it fall, while the appearance of security persists.

It is just as little to be supposed that these phenomena can be understood theologically, if one takes the word in the strict sense. Rather, one can presume that they will be manifest in every field to which belief is tied today, and therefore, especially, to the world of figures. And in fact we recognize that at the boundary where mathematics and the natural sciences meet, there are powerful changes underway. Astronomical, physical, biological conceptions are being transformed in a way that exceeds a mere change of theorems.

Admittedly, we still have not transcended the style of factories, although an important distinction emerges. The landscape of the factory, as we understand it, is essentially based upon a comprehensive obliteration of the old forms in favor of the greater dynamism of the process of work. The entire world of machines, traffic and war along with their destructions belongs here. In frightening images, like the burning of cities, obliteration reaches the highest intensity. Pain is immense, and nevertheless the form of the age is realized in the midst of the historical annihilation. Its shadow falls on the plowed earth, on the sacrificial ground. The contours of something radically new follow it.

The eye still reflects upon changes of decoration, which are distinguished from those of the world of progress and the Copernican consciousness. One has the impression that the ceiling no less than the scenery are coming nearer in a very concrete way and entering into a new perspective. One already anticipates that new figures will also take this stage.

Besides, no one will fail to see that in the world of facts, nihilism approaches its final ends. When we enter into its zone, only the head was endangered; the body, on the other hand, was still secure. Now it is reversed. The head is on the other side of the line. Meanwhile, the lower dynamism continues to mount, and builds toward an explosion. We live with terrifying hordes of missiles, calculated for the indiscriminate destruction of great parts of the human race. It is no accident that the same powers are at work here that discriminate against the soldier, who still understands the rules of combat and the difference between combatants and the defenseless.

Not that this process should be judged to be simply meaningless. It does not help at all to shut one's eyes in the face of it. It is an expression of the worldwide civil war in which we are involved. The enormity of powers and of means permits us to conclude that, at present, everything is at stake. Let us add to this the common characteristic of style. All of this points to the world state. It is no longer a question of the nation state, nor of territorial boundaries. It is about the entire planet.

This is one of the first signs of hope. For the first time a steady, objective purpose arises in the midst of boundless progress and its changes. And the will to attain it is not entirely a matter of power politics—it corresponds much more to the opinion that one hears on every street corner, in every railway compartment.

At the same time, the opinion spreads that a third world war, even if not inconceivable, is still not inevitable. It is not impossible that world unity could arise through treaties. It could be promoted by the rise of a third power, which would be conceivable in a united Europe. Too, the upheaval could attain a degree that will lead one of the rivals to fail within peace. Then there is the unforeseen. This urges upon all the judgment that with enough strength of spirit, neither optimism nor desperation is a given.

15

What to do in such a situation? Countless persons have brooded over this question. It is the theme of our age. It also does not lack an answer.

On the contrary, it is the sheer variety of answers that is confusing. Health does not arise when everyone is a doctor.

The true causes of our situation are unknown and are not illuminated by premature clarifications. These barely touch upon its secondary aspects. It could be that we judge too favorably. It could also be that the proximity of the disaster to us confuses the view and that later phases will shed more light on the epoch in its totality. That then would be a sign that nihilism is nearing its end. Perhaps before long one will see it in a completely different context.

In a similar way, knowledge of the remedy is limited. If we knew one great *arcanum*, the situation would lose its difficulty. Rather, it bears the mark of uncertainty, risk, fear, and every higher attempt to master them remains an experiment. On the contrary, we can assert that anyone who touts surefire prescriptions is either a charlatan or someone who has not yet noticed that the writing is on the wall. Whether in the sciences or elsewhere—*this* kind of assurance shows that what remains of the nineteenth century has not yet been entirely reduced.

On the contrary, one might very well recommend types of conduct, practical advice for negotiating the nihilistic terrain, since, in the end, there is no lack of experience. The free man is already obligated by reason of self-preservation to think about how he will behave in a world where nihilism not only rules, but, what is worse, has become the norm. That such a reflection has already become possible is the first sign of better, clearer weather, of a view that reaches further than the domain of powerful obsessions.

16

Regarding this perspective, it is necessary to mention something that must seem disturbing, or even inconceivable, to one who has not crossed these latitudes: namely, with the crossing of the equator the old figures are no longer valid, and a new calculation must begin.

This pertains especially to the inevitability of destruction. The conservative posture, whose representatives are worthy of respect, often worthy of admiration, is no longer capable of capturing and damming up the waxing movement, as still seemed possible after World War I. For the conservative must always rely upon areas not yet in motion, like the monarchy, the nobility, the army, the countryside. But when everything is in flux, the starting point is lost. Accordingly, one sees young conservatives defecting from static to dynamic theories: they encounter nihilism on its own ground.

This is a sign that things since the days of the old Prussian Marwitz have gone extremely far.[14] At that time it still might have seemed that only one granary, one barn was in flames. For widespread conflagrations other measures are necessary. Here one conceives a new plan.

There is no doubt that our situation as a whole is crossing over the critical line. With this, danger and security change. One can no longer think how to remove one house, one single property, from the path of the firestorm. Here no ruse, no flight can help. On the contrary—a whiff of absurdity clings to things saved in this way, or at best something museum-like. This also goes for intellectual matters; today it means little if a thinker maintains his point of view through the decades. Even development appears insufficient in these strange worlds—it is rather metamorphosis in Ovid's sense, mutation in the contemporary sense.

What figures are offered now to the mind that moves like a salamander through a fiery world? Here it sees images that associate themselves in an older way: it is impossible for them to stand fast, even if they lie in Tibet. There it sees the line where all values dissolve and where *pain* takes their place. Then he notices contours taking shape. They require above all sharp eyes; they can only be like germs, or like the core of crystals. And all these situations require another approach, which must appear muddled and completely contradictory to whoever cannot imagine both the negative and the positive side of annihilation. A Babel-like confusion divides the intellectuals, the theme of which is the exact location of the null point. Knowing this would certainly allow one to know the future system of coordinates.

A perspective is even possible where the line appears as a depth marker, as in an excavation. One penetrates to order by clearing away the rubble of ages and razing what the fellahs built. In this respect one sees strong minds serve the power of leveling inherent in nihilistic methods and terminologies. Here belongs the "Philosophy with a Ham-

---

14. Johannes Georg von der Marwitz (1856–1929), a Prussian cavalry general during the First World War, who commanded forces on both the Eastern and Western fronts.

mer," about which Nietzsche boasted, or the title "Demolition Expert" that Léon Bloy had printed on his calling card.

It remains vital to know to what extent the intellect submits to the necessary destruction and whether the march across the desert will lead to a new well. That is the task that our age harbors. Insofar as the solution depends on character, everyone takes a part in it. There is therefore a question of fundamental value, to which one must submit today's persons, works, and organizations. It is: to what extent have they passed over the line?

17

The confusion intimated above appears at first where one rightly supposes the heart of our difficulties, namely, in matters of belief. Its *supposition* is already a progress toward something better, compared to the total indifference of late Liberalism or worse. The catastrophes of the Second World War have made clear to many, even to the masses, an emptiness that they did not otherwise feel. That is the creative power of suffering, and such attempts at healing merit particular care and cultivation.

It lies in the nature of things that in such a situation the churches would be the first to provide a solution. That is their office, to which they are obligated. But immediately the question arises: how far are they capable of offering help, or in other words, to what degree do they still possess the means of salvation? The question is inevitable, since it is precisely uninspected edifices that could stockpile the material for an entrée of nihilism. Then what we described in the beginning would arise: the drama of prayer to which nothing transcendent corresponds, and which would then become an empty gesture, an automatic action like all the others—even lower, since it feigns value. That is the moment at which the rotation of a motor becomes stronger, more meaningful than the million-fold repetition of formulaic prayers. Many, whose eyes have been sharpened by nihilism, shrink back from such a repetition.

Posed in this way, the question does not remain in suspense long: it is foreseen. The moment in which the line is passed brings a new turning approach of Being, and with this, what is actual begins to shine forth. This will even be visible to dull eyes. New celebrations will follow.

On this side of the line, however, one cannot judge this state of affairs. We remain in the situation of nihilistic conflict, in which it is without doubt not only more sensible, but also more worthy to be on the side of the Church rather than on the side that attacks it. This fact has appeared only recently, and still appears today. After all, if canni-balism and enthusiastic worship of the Beast have not been instituted to the applause of the masses, we have the Church and a few soldiers to thank for it. At times, it was quite close to happening; and already beneath its banners their shone and shines still the splendor of Canaa-nite celebrations. Other powers scattered, all the more quickly the more socially and humanely they behaved. One should leave them to their bloodless decomposition.

The further forced retreat of the churches would either abandon the masses entirely to technical collectivization and its exploitation, or drive them into the arms of every sectarian and charlatan, who today play their games at every crossroad. This is the culmination of a century of progress and two centuries of enlightenment. One even hears the suggestion that the masses be left to their will, which drives them so clearly toward annihilation. This would make permanent the slavery in which millions languish and which exceeds the terrors of antiquity, but without its illumination.

We mention all this to avoid current confusions. We must then estab-lish that theology by no means finds itself in a condition capable of confronting nihilism. It fights much more against the rear guard of the Enlightenment, therefore finding itself entangled in the nihilistic discourse.

More hopeful is the fact that individual sciences on their own are moving toward images that are capable of a theological interpretation— above all, astronomy, physics and biology. They appear, after their expansion, to be approaching again a concentration, with a more restricted, sharper and therewith perhaps also more human view, pro-vided that one that conceives the word anew. Here one must guard against hasty interpretations; the results speak the most. New questions are still subjected to experiments. These also bring new answers. For their comprehension philosophy will not be sufficient.

The lack is least perceptible where worship suffices—in the orthodox core. It is perhaps the only thing able to cross the line without disinte-grating, or, if it disintegrates, it brings immense change. The lack will appear even stronger among Protestants than among Catholics; as a result, they will strive more energetically toward worldly activities and wellbeing. The decision should under no circumstance be taken away from the spiritual elites. All this leads to theological themes penetrating more starkly into literature. In France this hails back to an old tradition. An author's assimilation to and demarcation from the Church forms an unceasing conflict. The new exegesis leads to a debate between prophets and high priests, which, like that between Kiekegaard and Bishop Mynster, is repeated perpetually.[15] The theological novel, dismantled by Sterne, starts to appear again in Anglo-Saxon lands; now and again, even the same pens that still deal with the portrayal of the overman or with the last man devote themselves to it.

These three facts: the metaphysical discontent of the masses, the emergence of individual sciences from the Copernican realm, and the treatment of theological themes in world literature, are positive elements of high rank, which can justifiably be opposed either to a purely pessimistic assessment of the situation or to an assessment in terms of decadence. In addition there is a sort of élan, of simultaneously sober and energetic resolve, that could not be found with such clarity after 1918. It is encountered especially where suffering was greatest, and it distinguishes German youth. It is indeed more meaningful than victories, when after such a test one sees a return home from the ruins, from the pockets, from captivity.[16] There is no high spiritedness now, but in its place, a renewed courage to drain the cup grows. This weakens in the attack but gives immense forces to the resistance. They swell the ranks of the defenseless.

18

Today, where a readiness, a will to sacrifice, and therewith substance are manifest, the danger of meaningless waste always lies near. Exploi-

---

15. Jacob Peter Mynster (1775–1854) was a Danish theologian and Bishop of Zealand, Denmark. Søren Kierkegaard attacks him in his *Attack Upon Christendom*.

16. The word "pockets" (*Kessel*) alludes especially to the German army's encirclement at Stalingrad.

tation is the fundamental feature of the mechanical and automated world. It grows insatiably, when the Leviathan appears. One must not deceive oneself about this, when great wealth seems to gild its scales. It is even more formidable in times of comfort. The age of the monster state has begun, as Nietzsche foresaw.

Defeat is always deplorable. Yet it is not among those evils that lie entirely on the dark side; it even has advantages. Among them is a significant moral advantage, insofar as defeat excludes actions and therefore the shared responsibility connected with them as well. In this way a consciousness of right can grow that is superior to that of the protagonist.

One should not waive this and other advantages, only to involve oneself in questionable actions. Already the shadows of a new conflict fall upon our land. The German is attractive in the eyes of his enemies, not only because of the central location of his country, but also because of the elementary power concealed within him. This improves his situation and also brings new dangers. It forces him to deal from the bottom up with the problems that only from a rough point of view are political.

The confrontation with Leviathan, which imposes itself both as external and as internal tyrant, is the most comprehensive and universal in our world. Two great anxieties dominate men, as nihilism culminates. One is based upon fear of inner emptiness and compels man to manifest himself externally at any cost—through the development of power, control of space, and increased speed. The other works from the outside in as an attack of a powerful world simultaneously daemonic and automated.

The indomitability of Leviathan in our time rests in this duplicity. It is illusory; therein lies its power. The death it promises is an illusion, and *therefore* more terrifying than death on the battlefield. Even robust warriors are not equal to it; their mission does not lead them beyond the illusions. Hence the glory of arms must grow pale, where the ultimate reality, superior to appearance, is what counts.

If one succeeded in felling the Leviathan, it would still be necessary to fill the space cleared by its fall. In such a situation however inner emptiness, the state of unbelief, is incapable of assuming such a position. This is why when we see an effigy of Leviathan fall, new forms sprout like the heads of the Hydra. The emptiness demands them.

The same difficulty makes it impossible to prevent encroachments within the state directed against the individual. One can think of situations in which small elites would be allied, as in earlier times against the demos, in order to break the teeth of Leviathan and damage it. Its decline would then follow. We have experienced it. Similarly, parties would be conceivable or even sensible that would be armed to attack every bureaucracy that parasitically sucks the life from things. They could be assured of a majority, even of unanimous consent; it would change nothing. The creation of short-lived idylls would still be the best that could be expected. New centers would then form, unless Leviathan were simply to seize possession of easy prey from the outside, in order to leech out their substance more powerfully even than their own despots. It loves quietist ideologies and propagates them, but only alongside others.

Things are therefore not so simple. Astonishingly, even the man on the street sees it quite soberly; after all, he has paid the bill. The age of ideologies, still possible after 1918, has passed; they are little more than light greasepaint on the face of the great powers. Total mobilization has reached a stage that surpasses even the past in its power to menace. The German is clearly no longer its subject, and with this the danger grows that he is understood to be its object and after finishing his obligation is cheated of his wages.

Certainly, one cannot address this process simply by ignoring it. It demands a political attitude, the more urgent, the more one is defenseless—even if the political decision has been reduced and restricted only to the choice of a patron.

In addition, the supposition arises that all this is necessary and in the final analysis sensible. The formation of geopolitical spheres of influence and above all their increasing character of civil war indicates that it is no longer a question of the movement of nation states, but the preparation for a comprehensive unity, within which once more awaits a greater protection and a free life for peoples and fatherlands.

One of the chess moves of Leviathan lies in getting the youth to imagine that its summons is identical to that of the fatherland. In this way it recruits the best victims.

19

The path that grants neither internal nor external security is our path. Poet and thinker have described it more exactly, with greater awareness, with every new step. This is the path on which catastrophes loom ever more clearly and ever more immensely.

In such times of distress organization is offered to men. The word here is intended to compass its widest ambit, above all as order through knowledge and science. Economic, technical, political simplifications follow. It is impossible for men in this position to disdain the means that are offered them. Much is thereby taken from them, above all the agonizing decision, the personal choice. They also create security within this scope of order. Admittedly the immense number of decisions taken is concentrated in a few centers. With this, the danger of universal catastrophes appears.

It is foreseeable that the curtailment of freedom will last. It is also present when one naively imagines himself in possession of choices. Does it make a difference whether genocidal instruments are developed and stockpiled at the command of a tyrannical oligarchy or of a parliamentary vote? Certainly, there is a difference: in the second case the universal coercion is even clearer. Fear dominates everything, even when it reveals itself here as tyranny and there as destiny. As long as it rules, all is led about in an empty circle, and on their weapons rests a sinister light.

20

The question therefore arises, whether even a restricted field of freedom is still possible. Certainly, it is not given by remaining neutral—above all, not by any illusion of security, which undertakes to moralize to those standing in the arena.

Similarly, skepticism is not advisable, in particular, not any skepticism that is obvious. Minds that have administered doubt and profited from it have come a long way in the possession of power, and now doubting them is a sacrilege. They demand for themselves, for their doctrines, and for the Church fathers, an admiration that no emperor or pope ever claimed for themselves. Those who do not fear torture and forced labor can still run the chance of doubting. These will not be many. Acting so obviously renders to Leviathan exactly the service that suits it, for which it maintains armies of police. To recommend such action to the oppressed, behind the safety of the microphone, is purely criminal. Today's tyrants have no fear of the talking class. That may still have been possible in the good old days of the absolute state. Much more terrifying is the silence—the silence of millions and even the silence of the dead, that from day to day deepens and that no drumbeats manage to drown out, until it passes judgment. As nihilism becomes normal, the symbols of emptiness become more terrifying than those of power.

Freedom, however, does not dwell in emptiness, but lives much more in the disorderly and indiscriminate, in those areas that while capable of being organized, should not be considered organizations. Let us name them "the wilderness"; it is the space from which man may hope to lead to battle, even to victory. This then is clearly no longer a romantic wilderness. It is the original ground of his existence, the forest from which he will one day break out like a lion.

There are still oases in our deserts, where the wilderness blooms. Isaiah recognized this in a similar time of change. These are the gardens to which Leviathan has no access, around which he circles in rage. In the first place, there is death. Today as ever there are men who, not fearing death, are infinitely superior to the greatest temporal power. From this it follows that fear must be spread continuously. The despot always lives with the terrible thought that not only the individual but the many could rise above fear: this would be his sure downfall. Here too is the genuine reason for bitterness against every doctrine of transcendence. The greatest danger lies dormant there: that men become fearless. There are regions of the earth where even the word "metaphysics" is persecuted as heresy. It is self-evident that there, all admiration for heroes and for every great human figure must be dragged through the dust.

The second fundamental power is eros; when two individuals love, they seize ground from Leviathan, creating a space it cannot control. Eros will always triumph as the gods' true messenger over all titanic constructs. One will never fail when one stays by its side. In this connection let us mention the novels of Henry Miller—in them sex is a weapon against technology. It brings redemption from the iron chains of the age; turning to it annihilates the world of machines. The fallacy here lies in the fact that this annihilation is selective and must always be increased. Sex opposes nothing, but rather corresponds to the technical processes in the organism. On this level it is just as akin to the titanic as, for example, meaningless bloodshed, for the instincts are in opposition only when they drive one to love, to sacrifice. This sets us free.

Eros is also alive in friendship, which, confronted with tyranny, is subjected to the ultimate ordeal. Here it is purified and tested, like gold in the furnace. In times when suspicion penetrates into the family, the individual adapts to the form of the state. He arms himself like a fortress, from which no signs emerge. Where a pleasantry, even forgetting a gesture can mean death, great vigilance dominates. Thoughts and feelings remain locked within; one even avoids wine, since it awakens truth. In a situation like this, conversation with the trusted friend is not only infinitely consoling, but restores and affirms the world in its free and just measures. *One single* individual is a sufficient witness that freedom has not yet disappeared; but we need that witness. Then the powers of resistance awaken in us. Tyrants know this and seek to dissolve the human into the universal and the public—keeping at a distance everything unpredictable and extraordinary.

Freedom and the life of the Muses are inseparably bound together; it blossoms where the relation between inner and outer freedom is favorable. The creation of the Muses, that is, the work of art, still encounters enormous obstacles, inner and outer. This makes it even more deserving. Nothingness also sucks at the work of art, with immense power; this makes the creative act deliberate. One is in the habit of speaking of this as a deficiency, yet one should rather see it as the style of the times. Today, all creations of the muses, whatever the field, conceal a powerful dose of rationality and critical self-control—this is precisely what legitimates them, the sign of the time in which one recognizes their authenticity. Today, naïveté lies in other strata than it did fifty years ago, and what wishes to contravene the dream immediately succumbs to the cycle of mechanical reproduction. Today, we must train the conscious mind to be an instrument of redemption. For us it is the substance of the inexpressible, and even with our means it can raise its images to the rank of eternal value. Authenticity lies in limiting ourselves to what is given to us.

The meaning of art cannot be to ignore the world in which we live— and thus it has little serenity. Spiritual overcoming and command over the age will not reveal itself in the fact that perfect machines crown progress, but rather that the age gains a form in the work of art. In this way, the age is redeemed. Now it is true that the machine can in no way become a work of art, but the metaphysical impulse which animates the entire world of machines can receive in the work of art the highest meaning and in this way introduce rest into this world. This is an important distinction. Rest resides in form, even in the form of the worker. When one considers the path traversed by painting in this century, one will sense the sacrifices that are made here. One will perhaps also anticipate that it leads to triumph, for which the pure cult of the beautiful does not suffice. Besides, what is recognized as beautiful is open to debate.

A man can scarcely be found who would allow economics to dominate his garden to the point that one would not also find flowers planted there. The instant his flowerbeds bloom, pure necessity is surpassed. The man will have the same experience who in our order, in our states, turns, if only for an instant, toward the work of art. It may be that he can only approach it, as the Christian approaches the Cross, in the catacombs. In the sphere of Leviathan not only does bad style dominate; rather, an artistic person must necessarily be counted among its most significant opponents. Persecution is the mark of the artist. On the other hand, tyrants lavish praise upon those who enslave the spirit. They profane the poem.

21

It is similar for the thinker in this age. He courts the same risk at the frontiers of nothingness. It is why he *understands* the fear that men feel as panic and as blind strokes of fate. At the same time he approaches the salvation that Hölderlin sees accompanying danger.

One notes in this regard the curious symmetry that nowadays brings the poet and the thinker into mirror-like correspondence. Poetry has become conscious to a degree that surpasses all earlier attempts. The light penetrates into the web of dreams and primitive myths. To this belongs the increasing interest of woman in things of the spirit. On this side of the line it is one of the processes of reduction; only on the other side will it be clear whether the spirit profits from it, and in what way. If today an intelligent alien were to appear in the world, he could conclude from our poetry that we must possess knowledge of x-rays, and even of atomic processes. This was still not the case a short time ago, and it remains astonishing, if one thinks about it, how slowly the word follows the path of the spirit. In this way, the sun is always rising in language.

If in the poet language now mushrooms into the spheres of the spirit, in the thinker it sinks its roots into the undifferentiated. These are unmediated and complementary movements directly next to Nothing. This style of thinking is entirely different from that of classical ages like the baroque, where it was marked by the complete security, indeed the sovereignty of the absolute monarch. It can no longer even make the claim that positivism makes: that in every field in which intellect might proceed, pure consciousness and its laws dominates. The great tidal wave of the unknown has not only surpassed every level, but even the highest known watermark. Certainty in things of the spirit becomes questionable, even scandalous, like every inherited possession. Thinking must seek other assurances and recall other, more distant motives, like that of the gnostics, the pre-Socratics, or the hermits who settled in the Thebaid. New and yet very ancient leitmotifs emerge, such as anxiety. Nevertheless it is important to grasp that this thinking at the same time manifests distinct traits, inherited from the nineteenth century and its science. But where then do the definite and the indefinite meet—vagueness and precision? In many areas, as for example in experimentation.

And in fact the experimental belongs to the character of this thinking. For it is in fact the style that distinguishes not only painting, not only science, but even the existence of the individual. We seek mutations, possibilities, among which life in our new era could become possible, tolerable, even happy, perhaps. The scientific experiment directs its questions to the material world. We all know the incredible answers it has given that threaten the equilibrium of the world. This equilibrium can only be restored when thinking acquires answers from the spiritual cosmos that are superior to the material. The unique characteristic of our situation permits the conclusion that these acts of thinking must temporally precede theological propositions, even though they are oriented by them in advance—and perhaps not only thinking, but the trend of science in general, as a net in which other prey are caught than the ones expected.

Moreover, it is obvious that thinking, as we have inherited it, is insufficient for this. Nevertheless one cannot say that in thinking, as in general, an operation directed against the last century is carried out—its style, and in particular, its style of knowing, is rather extended and deepened. Admittedly, this style is also altered thereby, indeed, perhaps it becomes enormously more powerful—as even the onset of new material energies is based upon the learned work of our fathers. It is less a matter of operations and methods than of the responses of new powers. That allows us to suspect that from the start, the methods contained goals other than the intended ones.

Now we are in virgin territory. Here certainty is slim, but with greater hope of results. *Holzwege* is a beautiful, Socratic word for it.[17] It explains that we find ourselves off the beaten track and within an abundance of undifferentiated riches. As well, it embraces the possibility of failure.

22

The accusation of nihilism is among the most popular today, and everyone likes to deploy it against his opponents. It is likely that *all* are justified. We should then reproach ourselves, and not linger with those tirelessly on the search for culprits. He knows the age least who has not experienced the immense power of Nothing in himself and has not been tempted by it. The authentic heart: that is the center of the world of deserts and ruins, as was once in the Thebaid. Here is the cave besieged by demons. Here everyone stands, regardless of condition and rank, in direct and sovereign struggle, changing the world with their victory. If one prevails here, Nothing will recede. It will deposit treasures from the flood along the shore. They will compensate for the sacrifice.

OVERVIEW

1. Nietzsche's 2. and Dostoevsky's evaluation of nihilism. 3. The optimistic 4. and pessimistic judgment on nihilism. 5. Diagnoses of nihilism 6. surround the Nothing in the outer belt. 7. The relation of nihilism

---

17. The word *Holzwege* (*Forest Paths*) is the title for the first postwar book of Heidegger's; see GA: 5.

to chaos and anarchy, 8. to illness, 9. which is as untypical of it 10. as is crime. 11. Nihilism as the condition of decline 12. and of enchant-ment. 13. It leads back to figures and measurable conditions. 14. Nihil-ism approaches the last goals. 15. Under its spell there are ways of behaving, not means of salvation. 16. Within the change the question concerning the fundamental values can be posed only at the line, at the null meridian. 17. Attitude toward the churches 18. and Leviathan. 19. Organization and security. 20. Oases in the wilderness. 21. Thinkers and poets in this age. 22. The judicial power of the individual.

Index